The History of the Earth

Coen Nishiumi

Level 5

IBC パブリッシング

はじめに

　ラダーシリーズは、「はしご（ladder）」を使って一歩一歩上を目指すように、学習者の実力に合わせ、無理なくステップアップできるよう開発された英文リーダーのシリーズです。

　リーディング力をつけるためには、繰り返したくさん読むこと、いわゆる「多読」がもっとも効果的な学習法であると言われています。多読では、「1. 速く 2. 訳さず英語のまま 3. なるべく辞書を使わず」に読むことが大切です。スピードを計るなど、速く読むよう心がけましょう（たとえばTOEIC®テストの音声スピードはおよそ1分間に150語です）。そして1語ずつ訳すのではなく、英語を英語のまま理解するくせをつけるようにします。こうして読み続けるうちに語感がついてきて、だんだんと英語が理解できるようになるのです。まずは、ラダーシリーズの中からあなたのレベルに合った本を選び、少しずつ英文に慣れ親しんでください。たくさんの本を手にとるうちに、英文書がすらすら読めるようになってくるはずです。

《本シリーズの特徴》
- 中学校レベルから中級者レベルまで5段階に分かれています。自分に合ったレベルからスタートしてください。
- クラシックから現代文学、ノンフィクション、ビジネスと幅広いジャンルを扱っています。あなたの興味に合わせてタイトルを選べます。
- 巻末のワードリストで、いつでもどこでも単語の意味を確認できます。レベル1、2では、文中の全ての単語が、レベル3以上は中学校レベル外の単語が掲載されています。
- カバーにヘッドホーンマークのついているタイトルは、オーディオ・サポートがあります。ウェブから購入／ダウンロードし、リスニング教材としても併用できます。

《使用語彙について》
レベル1：中学校で学習する単語約1000語
レベル2：レベル1の単語＋使用頻度の高い単語約300語
レベル3：レベル1の単語＋使用頻度の高い単語約600語
レベル4：レベル1の単語＋使用頻度の高い単語約1000語
レベル5：語彙制限なし

Table of Contents

Introduction 2

1 The Beginning of the Earth 5

2 The Evolutionary Struggle
between Life and Earth 35

3 From Dinosaur to Human 61

4 Man Is a Thinking Reed 83

Word List 92

読み始める前に

【知っておくと便利な単語・フレーズ】

- □ ancestor
- □ carbon dioxide
- □ continent
- □ current
- □ crust
- □ evolve
- □ extinction
- □ fixed star
- □ fossil
- □ mammal
- □ mass
- □ meteor
- □ organism
- □ Solar System
- □ volcanic

【地球の大気圏】

【地球の構造】

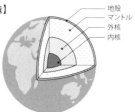

【太陽系の構成】

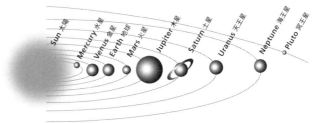

【地質時代区分】

Phanerozoic Eon 顕正代 (5億4200万年前~現代)	Cenozoic Era 新生代 (6550万年前~現代)	Quaternary Period	第四紀	ホモ・サピエンスの出現
		Neogene Period	新第三紀	
		Paleogene Period	古第三紀	
	---------- K-T boundary K-T境界線 ----------			
	Mesozoic Era 中生代 (2億5100万年前~6500万年前)	Cretaceous Period	白亜紀	恐竜の全盛期
		Jurassic Period	ジュラ紀	
		Triassic Period	三畳紀	
	Paleozoic Era 古生代 (5億4200万年前~2億5000万年前)	Permian Period	ペルム紀	
		Carboniferous Period	石炭紀	
		Devonian Period	デボン紀	
		Silurian Period	シルル紀	
		Ordovician Period	オルドビス紀	バージェス動物群の出現
		Cambrian Period	カンブリア紀	
---------- P-T boundary P-T境界線 ----------				
Precambrian Eon 先カンブリア紀 (46億年前~5億4200万年前)	Proterozoic Eon 原生代 (22億年前~5億4200万年前)	Neoproterozoic 新原生代	Ediacaran Period エディアカラ紀	植物の地上進出
			Cryogenian Period クライオジェニアン紀	
			Tonian Period トニアン紀	
		Mesoproterozoic 中原生代	Stenian Period ステニアン紀	
			Ectasian Period エクタシアン紀	多細胞生物の出現
			Calymmian Period カリミアン紀	
		Paleoproterozoic 古原生代	Statherian Period スタテリアン紀	
			Orosirian Period オロシリアン紀	
			Rhyacian Period リィアキアン紀	
			Siderian Period シデリアン紀	
	Archean Eon 始生代 (38億年~25億年前)	Neoarchean Eon	新始生代	
		Mesoarchean Eon	中始生代	
		Paleoarchean Eon	古始生代	
		Eoarchean Eon	原始生代	原始生命の出現
	Hadean Eon 冥王代 (46億年前~38億年前)			

The History of the Earth

Coen Nishiumi

Introduction

The English word "history," like the French word "histoire," means "story" or "account" —that is, a record of the past. Usually when we think about historical records, written accounts come to mind.

But the term "history" does not mean the actual words used to write the record. A "history" is the record itself. At one time, people engraved these records onto flat pieces of stone. In ancient China, people carved words on turtle shells, which were then heated to reveal a pattern that told them something about the future. They used these words both as a record and as a way to communicate with the gods of heaven and Earth.

What, then, does the "history" of the Earth mean?

The "history of the Earth" is a story written not in words, but in layers of rock, hidden fossils, flowers, molecules, and even our own

Introduction

bodies. It is an account of the past that normally is not heard.

By tracking these records, we are led back to the Earth, which gave birth to us, and then beyond to the universe, which gave birth to the Earth.

When we consider the history of the universe, it is natural to also consider the meaning of time. In the history of humanity, time starts in the past, reaches the present, and flows into the future. But there must be more to time than that, a mystery in the framework of the universe that streams in more than one direction. It may be that there is a hidden power beyond the edge of human thought, something that is pulling the strings of human history.

We human beings have called this power "god." The wonderful history of the Earth comes back to this idea, to which each of us is directly connected.

For English learners, this account of the Earth's history may contain math and science terms you have not seen before. As you follow the story of "Where did we come from and where are we going?" I hope you will get to know these terms so that you can express your thoughts in English about the matters discussed in this book. And whether your strengths lie in humanities or science, you'll learn the story of the road our ancestors have traveled for the last 4.6 billion years—and where we might go from here.

Coen Nishiumi
Autumn, Nasu Highlands

The Beginning of the Earth

The Life Span of the Earth

The universe and humanity have something in common: like us, stars are born, develop, grow old, and die. Although it seems to stretch forever, the universe and its countless stars will one day come to an end, or so it is said.

Sooner or later the Earth will also die. Scientists say that the Earth—which is currently at the height of its existence—is approaching the middle of its life. In about 4.5 billion years, the Earth will probably enter its final stage, as it disappears into the bright red flames of the sun.

In this book, we will follow the Earth's growth from birth to adult, and we will look ahead in the distant future, to its death. To continue to compare the Earth with human life, here are some important statistics.

- **Location:** Solar System, Orion Arm, Milky Way; third planet from the sun.
- **Birth:** 4.6 billion years ago.
- **Size:** The distance across the Earth is about 12,756 kilometers.

1 The Beginning of the Earth

Male or Female: The Earth is often called "she" in English. In French "Earth" is also a female word.

Family: Born as a child of the sun, the Earth's brothers and sisters are Mercury, Venus, Mars, Jupiter, Saturn, Uranus, Neptune, Pluto, and so on. (The search for other planets still continues.) The moon is the Earth's child.

The Beginning of the Universe

To explain the origin of the Earth, we must first examine the origin of the galaxies. The universe is said to have begun at the time of the Big Bang.

The Big Bang theory holds that the universe was in a very hot and dense state when an

Big Bang

explosion occurred. Due to this explosion, matter was blown apart and then drawn together, resulting in the forming of galaxies. As the explosion caused the universe to grow larger, the galaxies spread farther apart.

This theory is the result of the fact that bodies in space are always moving away from us. The speed with which such a body recedes and its distance from us are directly proportional. This law, which was discovered by American astronomer Edwin Hubble, forms the foundation of the Big Bang theory.

Scientists believe that the Big Bang occurred 13.7 billion years ago. However, this theory applies only to the universe as we know it; some say that there could have been another universe before the Big Bang. Also, the Big Bang can be viewed as just one stage of a continuing process. Perhaps, after the universe as we know it comes to an end, another Big Bang might occur.

Just as gravity causes a ball thrown into the air to come back down again, at some stage gravity might cause the universe to stop expanding. If that happens, the universe will contract back upon itself. This huge contraction would be called the Big Crunch. This theory is open to question.

What happens to the universe after repeated expansion and contraction? Many scientists have offered guesses, but no one has produced a clear answer.

The Birth of Our Solar System

About 9 billion years after the Big Bang, or 4.6 billion years ago, the solar system formed. One theory is that a star became a supernova and exploded. The resulting pieces became the sun and the planets. Another theory proposes that gravity caused material in various gas clouds floating in the universe to come together. This material created the celestial bodies that were the beginnings of our solar system.

A supernova is a huge explosion that occurs at the end of the life of a fixed star. Most fixed stars burn hydrogen. As a star's hydrogen levels reduce, the star begins to lose gravity. As a result, the energy the star lets out becomes greater than its gravity, and the star begins to expand.

When a fixed star grows to a certain point, the energy becomes stronger than the pull of gravity, and the star suddenly contracts toward its core. The explosion that occurs under the strain of this collision of forces is called a supernova. About 5 billion years from now, the sun will go through this process and meet its end as a fixed star.

In the early solar system, gas clouds containing hydrogen and helium must have turned in a spiral. Gravity caused the celestial bodies around the sun to draw together and collide with one another. The repeated process of collision and fusion caused large masses to form. The strong gravity of these masses attracted other large masses, leading to even bigger collisions. The largest masses became planets. The smaller objects continued to circle them.

The early Earth was born this way, as various celestial bodies circling the sun collided again and again. This mass of material drew in

1 The Beginning of the Earth

the gases that formed our atmosphere.

In time, a planetary body of equal size collided with the Earth; this collision is known as the Giant Impact. The impact stripped the Earth of its crust, melting it in the strong heat. Then, as the Earth gradually cooled, it became one clearly established celestial body. The Earth's increased gravity prevented the atmosphere from escaping into space.

Giant Impact

Gravity then pulled together the fragments of the Earth that had been sent flying into space by the Giant Impact. The resulting celestial body, under the influence of the Earth's gravity, began circling the planet. In that way, it could be said that the Earth gave birth to our moon.

The Sun Beats Jupiter

Jupiter

The planets in the solar system can be divided into those with a solid crust—from Mercury to Mars—and the "outer" planets formed mostly of gas, like Jupiter and Saturn. Jupiter is the largest planet in the solar system. At the time the solar system was formed and planets began to circle the sun, Jupiter was large enough to be a sun itself. But it did not have the mass to succeed. Instead, Jupiter went down in defeat to become a failed sun, a planet that now revolves around the sun like its brothers and sisters.

If Jupiter had somehow managed to draw in more gas and celestial bodies—and if it had grown larger than it is now—it would have changed places with the sun. Our solar system would be an entirely different place.

As the sun formed, the material drawn toward it by its gravity gathered at its center. The sun's interior pressure rose and its

1 The Beginning of the Earth

temperature increased. This led to a collision of hydrogen atoms, marking the beginning of hydrogen nuclear fusion. When the hydrogen underwent nuclear fusion, helium was the result, and a large amount of energy was released. The sun began to shine and has continued to do so. A fire had been lit in the stove of the sun.

The energy from an explosion spreads outward. As the sun reached a balance between the energy directed away from it and the pull of gravity back toward it, it entered a period of stability. Now, it could stay at a constant size. Finally, the sun had arrived at its final form as a fixed star.

The towering flames that rise up from the surface of the sun are called solar flares. Through these sudden bursts, very large amounts of X-rays and electromagnetic waves are let loose into space. When this magnetic energy reaches the planets, it is called the solar wind. At present, the sun lets out about 1 million tons of particles per second as solar wind. At its fastest, the solar wind reaches Earth at a speed of 900 km per second. The aurora that appears over the Arctic and Antarctic regions is a natural display of light that occurs when some of the solar wind reaches the Earth's atmosphere.

It is worth noting that the universe contains countless fixed stars like the sun, and their cosmic rays also reach the Earth. However, these cosmic rays are largely scattered by the solar wind.

If a huge explosion were to occur on the sun, the Earth would suffer greatly. The impact would be a magnetic storm. In the worst case,

aurora

1 The Beginning of the Earth

communication networks and power plants would be damaged. In its early history, the Earth was directly subjected to such solar winds accompanied by radiation. It was very difficult for life to develop on a planet that experienced those levels of radiation.

What happened after this? What caused life to come into being? Now let's take a look at the Earth in its childhood.

The Earth's Early Childhood

As we have seen, soon after its birth, the Earth was pretty well beaten up. But the Earth still somehow managed to endure—and to establish itself in the solar system as a real planet.

At the very beginning, the Earth's atmosphere was probably much like the sun's, consisting mostly of hydrogen and helium. The atmospheric pressure was high and the temperature was very, very hot.

Compared to the sun, the Earth was a baby. It was 1/109th the size of the sun, and only 1/330,000th the weight. Therefore, the Earth's core was not as hot as the sun's. So, after large collisions, the Earth's surface would turn molten before it started to cool again. When it became solid, it formed a crust that would cover the Earth with rock and soil.

Eventually, the Earth reached a size that allowed it to stay at a temperature that was friendly to life. At present, the oldest rock on Earth dates to 4.4 billion years ago, when the Earth's crust was formed.

When vapor in the air turned to rain, it fell to the ground and cooled the Earth's surface. Scientists think this was when the first seas developed. By examining ancient rocks, they believe that oceans formed about 4 billion to 4.3 billion years ago.

The collisions didn't end there, however. As you probably know, there are many craters on the moon. These are the result of meteor impacts. Scientists studying moon rocks have concluded that the moon and the Earth were subjected to many meteor impacts from about 4 billion to 3.8 billion years ago.

The reason for these impacts is unclear.

1 The Beginning of the Earth

One possibility is that as the solar system developed, it went through destabilized periods until the planetary orbits and the balance of gravity were settled. Meteors were always on the move.

Scientists have compared this period to a heavy bombardment. Some of these meteors were huge, measuring several hundred meters in diameter. So that you can better understand their impact, even the meteor that hit Russia in 2013 measured less than 18 meters—and it damaged buildings and caused injuries. The huge crater in South Africa known as the Vredefort Dome was caused by a meteor about 10 kilometers in diameter that fell 2.23 billion years ago.

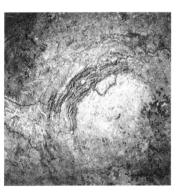

Vredefort Dome

The energy set loose by the impact shock of the meteors probably destroyed the Earth's crust, causing it to flow in waves like tsunami. The high temperatures caused the ancient seas to evaporate and the rock formations to melt, vaporize, and rise to the sky in violent currents of air. There they cooled, falling back down to Earth as a liquid much like lava. Under these conditions, whenever ordinary rain fell to Earth after cooling, it would heat up on the way down and again rise up as vapor. As a result, the surface of the Earth lost its water.

In a process that most likely took several thousand years, the Earth cooled down again, rain was able to reach its surface, and oceans once more came into being. This pattern occurred repeatedly over a period of at least 100 or 200 million years.

The Earth's gravity kept the meteor impacts from sending a great deal of matter into space. Instead, these various materials—both in and on the Earth as well as in its atmosphere—went through countless chemical reactions.

1 The Beginning of the Earth

The Earth Grows Up

The temperature at the center of the Earth is about 6000 degrees Celsius. This is equal to the temperature of the sun's surface. Compared to the sun, which at its core has a temperature of 15,700,000 degrees, the Earth is a cold place.

When the very hot material lying below the Earth's crust expands, it breaks through the crust and erupts onto the surface. This is how volcanoes are formed. Even before the period of meteor bombardment, carbon dioxide, carbon monoxide, ammonia, nitrogen, and water vapor were most likely let loose above the Earth's surface by the volcanic eruptions. The Earth's atmosphere formed from these materials. At the time, there was still no oxygen, an element necessary for human life. Some scientists believe that carbon dioxide entered the atmosphere because of meteors and other such objects.

Today, the atmospheric pressure on 1 square centimeter at zero sea level is considered to be

1 atm. In Earth's childhood, scientists believe that the planet was at more than 100 atm.

The large amounts of water vapor and other materials produced by volcanoes rose up into the atmosphere on air currents. When the atmosphere cooled, they fell back to the Earth as rain. Over long periods of time, the water accumulated and the oceans grew. The oceans were acidic, having absorbed sulfurous and hydrochloric acids in the atmosphere. Acid rain brought metallic ions into the ocean.

Most children are brought up by loving parents. That protective love is often warm and tender. But in order for a child to grow up to be an adult whom parents can be proud of, parents sometimes have to use tough love. That's what happened to Earth. While being rigorously tested by the universe, the Earth produced eruptions of hot magma, fierce lightning, and acid rain, like a child throwing a tantrum. So the universe—that stern parent—continued to test the Earth in a process necessary to produce a planet that could sustain life. Let's take a closer look at this process.

1 The Beginning of the Earth

The Hadean Era: Life Begins on an Angry Earth

The period of Earth's history before 540 million years ago is known as the Precambrian Era. We know very little about this time, which lasted 4.1 billion years. The Precambrian Era (and the Cambrian Period that followed) takes its name from the Latin word for Wales, the region lying in the southwest of Great Britain. That was where scientists discovered and studied the first rocks that had originated after the Precambrian Era.

The Precambrian Era is divided into three eras: the Hadean, Archean, and the Proterozoic Eras. During the Hadean Era, which covered the first 800 million years after the beginning of the Earth, violent natural events, including meteor bombardment, led to intense weather conditions. Static electricity caused countless thunderstorms.

Without these lightning strikes—without the anger of the Earth—life would not have come into being. We humans sometimes like to think of ourselves as the lords of all creation. We tend to place ourselves at the very top of life on Earth. And now, in order to keep our life of ease, we busy ourselves with attempts to control nature. The Japanese have long considered how they might bring earthquakes under control. The ancient Chinese tried to calm the Yellow River to improve their way of life. But it is exactly the uncertainty of nature, hated by humanity, that provided the driving force for the very existence of our ancestors.

Organic compounds are necessary to create life. In its earliest stage, Earth consisted of inorganic material made up of simple molecular structures. The air was mostly carbon dioxide. But the lightning's electricity set off a chemical reaction that combined complex organic compounds with carbon.

In his 1923 book *The Origin of Life*, Soviet scientist Alexander Oparin suggested that carbon and metal combined to form carbides, leading to a chemical reaction with vapor and ammonia in the atmosphere. This produced the first organic matter in the first oceans.

In 1953 Harold Urey and Stanley Miller proved this theory in what they called the

1 The Beginning of the Earth

Miller-Urey experiment. Miller and Urey used evaporated water to cycle methane, hydrogen, and ammonia—gases thought to be present in the Hadean Era—through glass flasks. When they introduced an electrical charge of 60,000 volts (the "lightning"), the chemical reaction created an amino acid. The amino acid, which is a more complex compound, combined further to produce protein. As this process was repeated, the reactions produced simple organic molecules: building blocks of life.

Scientists believe that ancient life began in the early oceans of the Hadean Era, accompanied by electricity in the form of lightning. These life forms probably favored conditions near volcanic vents under the sea. This was a location that was rich in minerals and most likely to be at a temperature near 100 degrees Celsius. A recent theory argues that chemical changes occurring near volcanic vents—particularly vents producing heated water—resulted in the creation of life. Among these life forms, it is further argued, some took shelter in areas several kilometers below the sea level.

Later, because of meteors, the oceans evaporated, making it impossible for life to exist anywhere near the Earth's surface. The result was that the only life managing to endure the rapid rise in temperature was that which had buried itself deep below sea level. In effect, our ancestors, to escape the heat above, spent several hundred million years deep in the Earth.

Then, about 3.8 billion years ago, the oceans formed once again and life returned to them. This period is called the Archean Era, which followed the Hadean Era.

The Archean Era: The Earth's Teen Years

The Earth somehow managed to live through its childhood and enter its teen years: the Archean Era, which lasted from 3.8 to 2.5 billion years ago. For people, the teen years are a time of psychological and physical unrest during which a child tries to develop into an adult. During Earth's teen years, it developed tectonic plates, the very foundation upon which the planet rests.

1 The Beginning of the Earth

As it passed through its childhood years, the Earth gradually began to settle down. Hot, thick liquids beneath the surface stayed there, surrounding the Earth's core in what is called a mantle. The hot liquids on the surface cooled off, producing a solid crust—the tectonic plates. Because the plates rest on the liquid mantle, they have the ability to move. When two of these moving plates crash into each other, the heavier plate moves under the lighter one. The shock of the impact is what causes earthquakes. The forward edge of bigger plates creates continents and mountains. The Himalayas were formed by the collision of the Indian plate with the Asian plate. The Great East Japan Earthquake of March 11, 2011, which had a magnitude higher than 9, was caused by the movement of such plates.

Scientists believe the plates were in the process of forming about 4 billion years ago as the earth was cooling. The first oceans and the Earth's early crust were destroyed by meteors. Only after the Earth once again started to stabilize did the plates, crust, and oceans of the present day come into being.

Plate movement has also had an important influence on the evolution of the Earth and its life forms. For example, the microorganisms that avoided the meteors by hiding deep in the Earth were carried back into the next round of oceans. Scientists think the movement of the plates played a part in this process. Naturally, the movement was very slow, at a rate of only a few centimeters a year.

As plate movement formed continents, the oceans stabilized, in time absorbing carbon dioxide but leaving nitrogen in the atmosphere. When the carbon dioxide thinned, the air itself became thinner, and atmospheric pressure approached what it is today. That's when life forms began to supply more oxygen.

The air today contains 80% nitrogen and 20% oxygen. It took considerable time for oxygen to reach that level. In order for that to happen, life forms had to be active near the surface of the sea or the land.

How did an Earth hit by so much radioactivity change itself into an Earth that was able

1 The Beginning of the Earth

to give birth to life? Another big development occurred in Earth's teen years. The Earth created a system to protect life forms, blocking out ultraviolet radiation and other harmful solar rays.

The Earth's core is made of iron, which can conduct electricity. Because the Earth moves, its liquid iron core has a fixed electric current. Since the electric current is accompanied by magnetism, the Earth has a magnetic field. This began during the Archean Era.

The effect of a magnetic field on life forms is huge. Thanks to its magnetic field, Earth was able to escape direct hits from the solar wind and its radiation, and life forms were able to move safely on the surface of the planet. One of the most important of these life forms was the blue-green algae called cyanobacteria, which appeared in the Archean Era.

A Note to Remember: Events of Long Ago Are Not As Distant As They Seem

We human beings know, of course, that individual lives are limited. All life ends in death. With some life forms, the time between birth and death is only a matter of seconds; with others, it can take more than a hundred years.

So, does death cut off all connections with future life? Well, when a mother gives birth to a child, life is passed from parent to child on a cellular level. Even if the individual dies, life is preserved by the cells and various microorganisms.

Consider genes. It is through genes that life has managed to evolve for billions of years. That is, even though life is limited on an individual level, its basic units are continually being passed on to life forms of the next generation. In that sense, as long as the Earth exists, life will continue to be passed on. From our ancestors born in the Hadean Era to more evolved life in the Archean Era, and finally to us today, the chain is unbroken.

1 The Beginning of the Earth

Today, human beings cannot live without oxygen. And there is also a limit to how much heat humans and most animals and plants can bear. However, the ancient life forms that passed genes down to us endured life in conditions quite different from ours. This can be seen in the Hadean and Archean Eras.

Today, some life forms exist that prefer to live near volcanic vents with temperatures of 100 degrees Celsius. Others live in areas without oxygen; they depend on nitrogen instead. These life forms show us how our ancestors adapted to the conditions of early Earth.

Put another way, we can now see that human beings, together with other mammals, are just a small part of the full range of life. However, we should also not forget that even the life forms that adapted to very different circumstances than ours faced the possibility of extinction following the Archean Era.

The Proterozoic Era: Snowball Earth

Let's take a look at what oxygen can do. When

oxygen reacts with methane, it is converted into carbon dioxide and water, as shown in the formula below.

$$CH_4 + 2O_2 \rightarrow CO_2 + 2H_2O$$

The carbon dioxide is further converted by photosynthesis into oxygen. At a glance, this process seems to create the perfect conditions for life. But in reality, it resulted in an important change that endangered life on Earth. This took place in the Proterozoic Era, the last age of the Precambrian Era.

Blue-green algae absorbed carbon dioxide, and, through photosynthesis, released oxygen. This is why there was an increase of oxygen on Earth. When the algae died, the carbon converted from carbon dioxide settled at the bottom of the ocean onto a tectonic plate. Over a long period of time, these materials sunk deeper into the Earth through holes in the Earth's crust. As more and more carbon dioxide sunk underground, the carbon dioxide in the air was reduced.

1 The Beginning of the Earth

What effect did this have on Earth? Carbon dioxide plays a role in keeping the heat from the sun on the Earth's surface. If the amount of carbon dioxide declines, the heat from the sun's radiation is lost into outer space, and the temperature of the Earth drops. That's what happened about 2.4 billion years ago: Earth's temperature began to fall.

Over a period of tens of millions of years, this change gradually affected our planet. As the temperature fell, the ice at the two poles began to grow and move south. When the Earth started to turn white, the sun's rays were reflected off the ice, further speeding up the cooling. In time, the entire planet was covered in ice in what is now called "Snowball Earth."

This ice age, the earliest that we know of, is called the Huronian glaciation. Specialists who study the history of the Earth think that the planet was completely frozen for tens of millions of years. The temperature at the poles was -90 degrees Celsius. The temperature along the equator dropped below -50 degrees

Celsius. On land, the ice was about 3,000 meters thick.

On Snowball Earth, life forms near the surface probably became extinct. Scientists believe the blue-green algae managed to survive by attaching itself to areas with high temperatures near volcanic vents, hiding down there for years.

What finally saved Snowball Earth was volcanic activity. Eruptions caused the underground carbon dioxide to return to the air.

The Huronian glaciation is said to have ended 2.1 billion years ago. But the battle between life forms and the world around them continued. Earth completely froze over two more times: during the Sturtian glaciation (about 760 million years ago to 700 million years ago) and the Marinoan glaciation (about 620 million years ago to 550 million years ago).

After the first Snowball Earth, the planet's temperature experienced a sudden increase. With the rise in temperature, convection air currents became active, and the Earth was hit

1 The Beginning of the Earth

by large-scale storms with typhoons, winds, and lightning. When the seas grew tempestuous, the water stirred up minerals from within the Earth. Blue-green algae and other microorganisms grew well. As oxygen increased, life forms became more active, and some began to evolve by mutation. Then, about 2 billion years ago, the eukaryote appeared, a life form with a complex structure and a cellular nucleus.

In this nucleus, DNA could be safely stored and genetic information preserved. Gradually, the DNA was copied and protein was synthesized by RNA, a process close to what we have today.

To put it another way, when cell division occurred, DNA was passed on by chromosomes, making the evolution of higher life possible. It took nearly 3 billion years to reach this stage, but the effect was striking. Fossils show that by the end of the Precambrian Era, after the Marinoan glaciation, large-scale plant life and primitive animals came into being.

2

The Evolutionary Struggle between Life and Earth

The Mission of Cells in the Evolution of Life

While the first 3 billion years of evolution was slow, the next billion years moved quick as a flash. After Snowball Earth thawed, living things began ravenously absorbing the Earth's abundant carbon dioxide, much as a starving wolf might attack a group of cattle. The most primitive life, which consisted of a single cell, began to divide and multiply. This evolution toward multicellular life began about 1 billion years ago. In multicellular organisms, each cell has its own special function. This makes it possible for certain cells to develop into internal organs, for example.

As cells became more specialized, life forms could increase their range of activity. For 1 billion years after the appearance of multicellular organisms, living things experienced a rush of evolution that would eventually lead to human beings.

The Rise of the Supercontinent

As life forms evolved, what changes did the land and seas undergo?

"Plate tectonics" is the theory that plates riding on the Earth's mantle undergo lateral movement. Plate tectonics was discovered fairly recently, in the 1960s.

Land masses probably first appeared in the Precambrian Era when the Earth cooled somewhat and the oceans receded. Volcanic activity also played an important role in forming considerable amounts of land. Scientists think these land masses, which were moved by tectonic plates, collided with one another until they formed supercontinents.

The mantle was an important part of the forming of the continents. At the spot where plates riding on the mantle descended into the Earth, matter with a high relative gravity moved farther down and was melted by the mantle. Matter with a low relative gravity, like granite, began to build up, gradually appearing on the ocean's surface and developing into a continent.

As more and more matter accumulated at these cracks in the Earth, scientists believe that continents formed that were much larger than any that exist today—supercontinents. This theory is supported by the way that fossils are spread around the world.

The oldest known supercontinent is the Nuna continent, which formed about 1.9 billion years ago. This huge continent is thought to be the predecessor of the continents of North America, Greenland, and most of Europe.

Consider what happens when you heat a large beaker of water. As the beaker is heated, the hot water rises until it reaches the top. Then it flows to the sides of the beaker and cools. The cooler water sinks to the bottom.

The same type of thing happens when the mantle is heated by the Earth's central core. You can now understand how the mantle flows down and plates collide and sink. Land masses are formed from the matter that builds up on the surface rather than sinks.

Of course, just as with water directly above

2 The Evolutionary Struggle between Life and Earth

a flame, the mantle directly above a source of heat rises with such power that it breaks apart whatever is above it. This, in fact, can explain how supercontinents could break apart, so it deserves a closer look.

Once a supercontinent is created, material like granite continues to accumulate. On the surface, mountains develop. Inside the Earth, huge sections of magma form. Some of them are shaped like a mushroom. When these mushrooms reach a certain size, they break off from the continent and, as a drop of rain might fall to the ground, they sink through the liquid mantle toward the Earth's core. This causes hot, powerful magma—called a "plume"—to push up toward the surface of the Earth, reversing the convection currents of the magma. That energy breaks up the supercontinent into separate pieces, which begin to move on their own.

This theory of mantle convection currents is called plume tectonics.

The Earth Is Changing and Will Continue to Change

Earth might now be attempting to gather these pieces into a supercontinent once again. In the next 150 million years, scientists say that Africa will connect to Europe, and the Mediterranean will disappear. Australia will join with China and Southeast Asia. And the sea to the north of Indonesia will become a lake surrounded by land.

It is a pattern: A supercontinent breaks into individual continents and then gradually forms again as a supercontinent. The Earth might have repeated this pattern many times since the Nuna supercontinent formed. For example, India separated from the Antarctic continent and collided with the Eurasian continent. As mentioned earlier, this collision created the Himalayas, as well as the Tibetan Plateau, in their current forms.

There have been periods when Earth had two supercontinents at the same time. Each was brought together by the Earth's mantle

2 The Evolutionary Struggle between Life and Earth

and each was later torn apart by it. These supercontinents included Columbia (formed 1.8 billion years ago), Pannotia (1.5 billion years ago), Rodinia (1 billion years ago), Pangaea (250 million years ago), Gondwana (which existed from 600 million to 100 million years ago), and Laurasia (from 200 million years ago to 60 million years ago). The continents from Rodinia on, in particular, were formed by the pattern of continents colliding together and breaking up.

Let's return to the last 10 million years or so of the Precambrian Era, 35 million years after Snowball Earth. At that time, a variety of mollusks appeared that do not exist today. Scientists found fossils of these types of mollusks in Ediacara, South Australia and named the group as a whole—which scientists call a "biota"—the Ediacara biota. The Gondwana supercontinent was in the process of forming. The Earth was getting warmer.

As the Earth warmed, the oceans grew wider, covering the edges of the continents and creating many continental shelves. Conditions

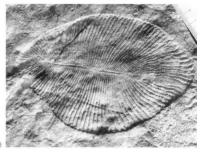
Ediacara biota

were friendly for living things, with plenty of sun and oxygen. Life on earth continued to grow.

Earth Becomes an Adult: Life Moves Onto Land

The movement of continents on the mantle sometimes gave rise to large, shallow seas. These waters, surrounded by land, were also helpful to life on Earth.

However, in order for life forms to make their way onto land, another important condition had to be met. There had to be a change in the upper level of the Earth's atmosphere, that is, the development of an ozone layer.

2 The Evolutionary Struggle between Life and Earth

As the growing number of life forms increased the amount of oxygen on Earth, particles of ultraviolet light from the sun struck oxygen molecules, which changed into ozone, as follows:

$$3O_2 \rightarrow 2O_3$$

Ozone is a toxic gas with powerful oxidizing properties. In the atmosphere it absorbs ultraviolet light, splitting oxygen molecules into oxygen atoms. This stops some of the ultraviolet radiation from reaching the Earth's surface.

In the air above the Earth, ozone was steadily pushed up into the higher layers of the atmosphere. At present, the Earth has a thick ozone layer 10 kilometers to 50 kilometers up in the stratosphere. This prevents short wavelength ultraviolet light from irradiating the Earth.

The fact that short wavelength ultraviolet radiation is used as a disinfectant suggests its power to destroy living things. For example, if the skin of a living organism is irradiated, the collagen fiber in the skin is seriously damaged; this can cause cancer and other illnesses. In fact, if the Earth had not developed a magnetic field or an ozone layer, life forms could not have safely evolved and made their way onto the Earth's surface.

The ozone layer began to develop just as the Huronian glaciation came to an end, scientists believe. It developed enough to energize life forms by the last stage of the Precambrian Era, around the time the Ediacara biota appeared.

The forming of continents by the movement of the Earth's crust, the rise of the sea level, and the development of the ozone layer: What were the chances that these three things would happen? Without them, our ancestral life forms would not have been able to evolve.

As multicellular organisms continued to evolve, plants living at the water's edge, such as liverworts (Marchantiophyta) and ferns, began to move onto land about 500 million years ago. In time, plants developed roots, stems, and leaves.

2 The Evolutionary Struggle between Life and Earth

About 350 million years ago, during a warm period, the Earth first became covered with vegetation. Forests grew rapidly, and photosynthesis increased the oxygen in the air, which encouraged even more growth. Now, for the first time in the more than 4 billion years since its birth, the once dull brown planet became a rich bright green.

As ancient trees in swamps and other areas died out, they were carbonized in the water and turned into coal, an important source of energy. During the Carboniferous Period, from 359.2 million to 299 million years ago, vegetation grew that would later become coal.

In order for animals or plants to evolve, the genetic information in the DNA within the cell nucleus has to be copied and passed on to the next generation, including errors that occurred in the copying process. In other words, any mutations that occur are also transmitted to the next generation. For plants to live on the land—and, in particular, to endure its dry conditions—they needed evolutionary structural changes. They needed a system to supply and preserve water and nutrition with roots, stems, and leaves.

What's more, in order for life to advance on land, simple cell division was not enough. Plants needed to form seeds, which the wind would spread. Seeds are the result of fertilization of pistils and stamens. They are a new individual organism, that is, an embryo wrapped in a covering. This means of reproduction was first developed by ferns—and a new system was born.

Animals Join Plants on Earth

How did animals come into being?

Here we have to turn the clock back to the Precambrian Era. Of particular interest to scientists are the choanoflagellates, living organisms found in single-cell life forms.

For living things to evolve as multicellular organisms, they need a substance that will encourage the cells to

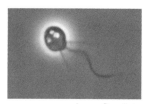

choanoflagellate

2 The Evolutionary Struggle between Life and Earth

attach to each other. This substance is the choanoflagellate. The first multicellular animals to appear on Earth were most likely the sponges. They are made up of a primitive digestive organ and choanocytes with flagella. These multicellular animals managed to live through the 100-million-year snowball period by living near volcano vents.

When the Earth grew warmer, the species that were left on the planet experienced a strong period of evolution. We can see signs of this in the fossils of the Ediacara biota. Similar fossils have been found near the White Sea in Russia, South Africa, and southern China.

The animals of the Ediacara Period lived in the water. As the number of predatory animals that were their natural enemies increased, they came close to the edge of extinction. This brings us to the end of the Precambrian Era.

As the Precambrian Era ended and the Cambrian Period began, the formation of supercontinents like Gondwana created shallows and continental shelves. Because of this development, protozoa evolved in places where there had been only limited life forms. A variety of metazoan life appeared with connections to the present day.

Fossils of the predecessors of these animals, a group called the Burgess Shale biota, have been discovered in the Canadian Rockies. Similar fossils were found in Yunnan province in China.

The period from 510 million to 439 million years ago is called the Ordovician Period. During this time, which followed the Cambrian Period, mollusks appeared, such as nautiluses, arthropods, and trilobites.

Scientists believe the first animals to live on land appeared in the Silurian Period, which came after the Ordovician Period. The first animals to make their way onto land were the arthropods.

trilobite

nautilus

2 The Evolutionary Struggle between Life and Earth

Life Evolves Against All Odds

Why did animals accomplish such impressive evolutionary progress? In order for life forms to evolve, they must be faced with a challenge that their current form cannot handle. As the Earth endured quakes and eruptions, meteor showers, and complete freezes, its life fought off extinction and continued to evolve.

Much of the creatures' success was an accident, of course. Genetic mutations produced stronger life forms that managed to endure difficult conditions, passing the flag of life to the next generation.

Gradually, the vertebrates appeared. Some of them were descendants of a type of land slug that was later discovered in the Burgess Shale biota. Scientists believe this discovery helps to validate the theory of evolution.

When fish with vertebrae appeared, their predatory activity most likely caused the development of a food chain. For the life forms near the bottom of the food chain, this was not good news. They had to learn how to quickly escape their enemies, to grow protective shells, or to develop other means of survival. This is why creatures began to develop legs for speed and a skull to protect the central nerves of the brain.

Finding food in the water was easy; minerals were readily available. But to live on land, creatures needed to be more active and to be able to store nutrients within the body. Therefore, to both strengthen their bodies and to store what they needed to, animals developed bones. This framework for the body first appeared at least 400 million years ago at about the same time the most famous of all fossils, the ammonites, first came into being.

There was still one more piece missing that was necessary for creatures to increase their range of activities from ocean to land: a way to breathe outside of the water. Lungs.

The first species to develop lungs was the *Eusthenopteron*, a fish that appeared 380 million years ago, in the Devonian Period of the Paleozoic Era. Ranging from 30 to 120 centimeters long, this fish lived in shallow

2 The Evolutionary Struggle between Life and Earth

waters, where they developed a system of lung breathing to take in oxygen more efficiently.

With this development, the stage was set for the vertebrates to make their way onto land. About 360 million years ago, around the beginning of the Carboniferous Period, the ancestors of the vertebrate Ichthyostega, which lived on land, first appeared. The *Eusthenopteron*, fish that could breathe through lungs, began to grow legs instead of fins, which enabled them to be active on land. The *Ichthyostega* developed ribs to protect their lungs.

At this time, the Earth was warm. Plants living at the water's edge began growing onto land, where they grew well because of the rise of oxygen density in the air. Now that animals were able to breathe this oxygen, too, they also made their way onto land. As vertebrate organisms like the *Ichthyostega* also appeared on land, the Earth suddenly became a very busy place.

Mass Extinctions Challenge Life on Earth

Even though plants and animals had become well established on land, the path to human life was not easy. The Earth still had a few tricks that it had not yet revealed. Fossils and rock layers indicate that at least five mass extinctions took place following the first appearance of multicellular organisms.

The first mass extinction that we know of occurred in the Proterozoic Period at the end of the Precambrian Era, about 345 million years ago. Life forms such as the mollusks in the Ediacara biota became active at the end of the Precambrian Period and then suddenly disappeared. The question of whether all life became extinct at this time has not yet been answered, but there is no doubt that a mass extinction occurred.

The cause of this extinction was probably the magma countercurrents—which are a part of plume tectonics—on the Gondwana supercontinent. Magma mushrooms lying below the Earth's surface suddenly plunged into the

2 The Evolutionary Struggle between Life and Earth

mantle. The impact caused a huge amount of magma to rush up to the surface; this is called a superplume. Volcanic super-eruptions forced out gas and magma from below the crust onto the surface of the planet. Volcanic ash covered the Earth and the air, cutting off the light from the sun. The Earth's temperature suddenly dropped. The Ediacara biota died out.

Later, because carbon dioxide had returned to the atmosphere, the temperature began to rise again. In the Cambrian Period, the first period of the Paleozoic Era, primitive animals began to evolve once again. Multicellular metazoans appeared. Then, 444 million years ago, during the Ordovician Period, a supernova exploded close to Earth. Large amounts of gamma rays showered the planet.

Gamma rays are dangerous because they are a type of electromagnetic radiation. Scientists believe that this explosion destroyed many life forms, including 85% of the trilobites that had managed to grow well even after the mass extinction of the Ediacara biota.

About 375 million years ago, during the

Devonian Period, the Earth was finally covered in green again. The oceans were home to a wide variety of life, such as the ancestors of cartilaginous fish including sharks and rays. At the top of the ecosystem was a fish called the *Dunkleosteus*, which grew to six meters in length. This period is known as the Age of Fish.

But this group of organisms suddenly suffered a major drop in numbers. Some scientists believe that changes in the ocean currents played a part in the mass extinctions of ocean life at this time.

Until then, the warm water around the equator was cooled near the North and South Poles. The cooled water circulated near the ocean floor, supplying oxygen to the creatures at the lower levels of the sea. When the Earth warmed, however, the ice at the poles began to melt. The ocean currents could not circulate as easily. This situation is called an oceanic anoxic event.

That's what happened in the Devonian Period. With the lack of oxygen, many creatures could no longer live, which had a major effect on the food chain. At the same time, heavy rains washed organic matter into the ocean. This caused an explosive growth of plankton on the continental shelves. The carbon dioxide in the air rapidly ran out. The planet cooled.

The event was like a smaller Snowball Earth. Scientists think that this smaller snowball led to a mass extinction, destroying species such as the *Dunkleosteus*. After this mass extinction, the shores were probably colored red with plankton.

But the mass extinctions did not end there. About 251 million years ago life on Earth experienced perhaps its cruelest blow. More than 90% of all living things were wiped off the planet. There are a number of possible reasons for this event, but we will take a closer look at one: volcanic activity.

In northern Siberia there are vast layers of basalt called the Siberian Trap; they are what is left from a huge volcanic explosion. A magma mushroom fell into the lower depths of the supercontinent Pangaea, which was then in the process of forming. The superplume that resulted caused the volcano to erupt. It continued to erupt for more than a million years. The rapid warming of the Earth and the decline of oxygen was a death sentence for most life forms. Some that had barely escaped other mass extinctions, such as the trilobites, were completely destroyed at this time.

This is just an overview of four of the times when mass extinction threatened life on Earth. Before, after, and in between these events, other changes also tested life on Earth. We can see how fierce the Earth has been at sorting out life forms. We humans are the descendants of organisms that were repeatedly tested by challenge after challenge and, almost unbelievably, managed to survive.

Then again, let's say that a mass extinction occurs every 50-75 million years. That means mass extinctions are not just events of the past. They could also happen in the future. For all we know, we humans may be nothing more than a life form that has managed to evolve

2 The Evolutionary Struggle between Life and Earth

and thrive between periods of mass extinction.

The Evolution of Breathing

In its childhood years, early Earth struggled to reach a physical form that could stand the test of time. When living organisms appeared as part of that process, by the very act of living, they created an environment that further influenced the Earth.

When the Earth caught a cold or trembled with fever, living things were again threatened by mass extinction. One accident followed another, and some life forms were lucky enough to find their own means of evolving. It was these forms that built the foundation on which the following generations would grow and develop. As the patterns of natural selection and evolution repeated, life forms developed more advanced survival systems.

Which life forms were able to continue to evolve? When the atmosphere ran out of oxygen because of the superplume events at the end of the Permian Period, the organisms that were left adapted in clever ways.

You may know the phrase "athlete's heart." It occurs when an athlete's heart grows bigger because he or she requires large amounts of oxygen. This condition is not a matter of genetics. It can best be described as a physical adaptation by the individual organism. If oxygen levels were to decline on Earth today, humans might evolve to adapt to the change. They might begin by genetically passing on the athlete's heart.

In much the same way, when life forms struggled to overcome the difficult trials of the Permian Period, they gave themselves a more efficient system of breathing. This new system allowed them to be active in areas with low oxygen.

A classification of animals known as the archosaurs showed an impressive development after they first appeared in the late Permian Period. (Descendants of archosaurs included crocodiles, dinosaurs, and even birds.) Archosaurs developed an air sac, a respiratory organ that helps the lungs. By expanding

2 The Evolutionary Struggle between Life and Earth

and deflating, the air sac makes the intake of oxygen much more efficient.

Another classification of animals that increased the efficiency of their breathing was mammals. Mammals developed a diaphragm under the lungs to make abdominal breathing possible. It should be noted, however, that, in these early years, the breathing efficiency of mammals was far inferior to the archosaurs and their air sacs.

By improving their respiratory organs, some animals were able to endure the cruel mass extinction of the Paleozoic Era. As living conditions improved and the amount of atmospheric oxygen recovered, these animals quickly evolved. Some species went on to reach

gigantic proportions. These, of course, were the dinosaurs.

After the mass extinctions of the Paleozoic Era, the Earth entered the Mesozoic Era (250 million years ago). This brings us to the time when mammals and reptiles would fight it out for superiority.

3

From Dinosaur to Human

The Triassic and Jurassic Periods: The Beginning of the Dinosaurs

The Mesozoic Era can be divided into the Triassic, Jurassic, and Cretaceous Periods. The geological term "P-T boundary" comes from the first letter in "Permian" Period—which preceded the Triassic—and the first letter in "Triassic" Period. The P-T boundary is the line between the Paleozoic and Mesozoic Eras.

Life forms that endured the huge mass extinctions of the Permian Period made it to the Triassic Period, which is the reason that scientists pay particular attention to conditions before and after the P-T boundary. For example, an archosaur called *Thecodontosaurus*, which lived in the latter half of the Triassic Period, stood from 1 meter to 2.5 meters tall. The carnivore *Coelophysis* reached 2.7 meters in height. Both were early dinosaurs.

Atmospheric oxygen levels in the Triassic Period were still low. That's why it took nearly 100 million years for dinosaurs to reach huge proportions, the amount of time that lasted

3 From Dinosaur to Human

from the Triassic Period to the Jurassic Period.

At this time, land masses had just come together to form one supercontinent, Pangaea, which was surrounded by an ocean called Panthalassa. To the east of the continent was a large bay called the Tethys Sea. In this bay and on the continental shelves, new forms of sea life evolved. They included a new type of ammonite, sea urchins, sea lilies, and other types of echinoderm, as well as ichthyosaurs, which were somewhat similar to today's dolphins.

Along with the ancestors of the dinosaurs, life forms such as the amphibians and reptiles also grew well, and the Earth was full of ferns and common liverworts. Synapsids, a distant relative of mammals, were also common.

At the end of the Triassic Period, Pangaea began to break apart. Between the resulting increases in volcanic activity and meteor impacts, many of these organisms again suffered mass extinction.

Some archosaurs with more advanced respiratory organs endured this challenge to become the huge dinosaurs of the Jurassic Period. This period occurred from 199 million years to 145 million years ago.

In the Jurassic Period, Pangaea, which had already begun to break up, divided into the Gondwana and Laurasia supercontinents. Laurasia broke apart into the masses that would become the North American and Eurasian continents. From Gondwana the new continents of Antarctica, Australia, Africa, and South America formed.

The climate in the Jurassic Period was subtropical. In the heat and humidity, trees like pine trees, palms, and king sago began to grow. Mammals that were similar to rats—and other plants and animals familiar to us today—began to appear in the lands of the dinosaurs. And then, toward the end of the Jurassic Period, about 150 million years ago, the first bird, the *Archaeopteryx*, took wing.

3 From Dinosaur to Human

The Cretaceous Period: The Golden Age of Dinosaurs

The Cretaceous Period covered the stretch from 140 million to 65 million years ago. It was warm and very humid, a perfect climate for both plants and animals. There were no movements of the Earth's crust that could threaten mass extinctions. Dinosaurs and reptiles wandered freely.

The Cretaceous Period, which followed the Jurassic, was truly the golden age of dinosaurs. Fossils discovered in North America show that the carnivorous *Tyrannosaurus*, which is often seen in movies, appeared at this time. The *Tyrannosaurus* reached a height of more than 11 meters. With its powerful jaws and teeth, it preyed on other dinosaurs. There was a large variety of dinosaurs, ranging in size from tiny creatures to animals that weighed more than 50 tons. Among the dinosaurs that ate only plants

Tyrannosaurus

was a member of the Brachiosauridae family that was 25 meters long, 16 meters tall, and weighed close to 80 tons.

As far as the food chain was concerned, herbivorous animals did well because plants were easy to find. Animals that ate meat had plenty of prey. Conifers and fig trees began to grow. In fact, the areas of vegetation were much as they are today.

In the Cretaceous Period, mammals made unprecedented evolutionary advances. Our mammal ancestors, the synapsids, are also considered mammal-like reptiles. The most common synapsids were the cynodonts, which were widely active on Pangaea beginning in the Permian Period.

While most of the cynodonts disappeared in the mass extinction at the end of the Permian Period, some managed to live on. So did the Thrinaxodon, which is thought to be one of our direct ancestors. About 50 centimeters in length, the Thrinaxodon fed on small animals. Its ribs, like ours, covered the chest area but not the abdomen. This enabled abdominal

3 From Dinosaur to Human

breathing and activity in areas with low oxygen levels. The first genuine mammal, the *Adelobasileus*, appeared in the latter half of the Triassic Period, about 225 million years ago.

As mentioned earlier, mammals later developed a diaphragm that increased breathing efficiency by expanding the abdomen. Because of this development of the abdomen, mammals gradually developed the means to give birth live instead of laying eggs. This probably happened around the beginning of the Cretaceous Period.

Mammal mothers could now feed the fetus and keep it safe, from the fertilization of the egg to its birth. Because of these changes, the synapsids gradually evolved into the mammals that we know today. Most mammals then were the size of rats. They were active at night, running around to keep out of the way of the dinosaurs.

In the Cretaceous Period, mammals, many kinds of reptiles, dinosaurs, and birds were active on land and along the water's edge. The plant kingdom also saw new developments. Along with the many plants that spread by spores, there was an increase of seed plants that reproduced by developing flowers and a system of pollination.

Size Doesn't Matter: The Dinosaurs Meet their End

65 million years ago this paradise was destroyed. While there are many possible causes, the most likely reason the dinosaurs died out was the impact of a huge meteor. This meteor, 15 km in diameter, created the Chicxulub Crater in what is now the Yucatán Peninsula. The impact likely caused an earthquake of magnitude 11 or higher and a tsunami several hundred meters tall that flooded the land. And worst of all, dust must have risen into the Earth's atmosphere, blocking the rays of the sun and leading to a cooling of the planet.

Some scientists believe that the Earth could have been hit by a number of meteors in a short period of time. They present as evidence the fact that iridium, which indicates a meteor

3 From Dinosaur to Human

impact, has been found in layers of rock in various locations across the planet.

Others believe that a meteor impact cannot sufficiently explain the extinction of the dinosaurs. The truth, however, is still a puzzle.

One thing seems certain, though. In order to sustain their huge bodies, the dinosaurs required considerable sources of energy. If for some reason the food chain balance was broken, these creatures would rather quickly find themselves wiped out once and for all.

What did the extinction of the dinosaurs teach us? We can see that it is possible that life forms can adapt too closely to their environment. The ancestors of the dinosaurs learned to live in areas with low oxygen levels and they lived through the mass extinction of the Permian Period. The dinosaurs learned to live in changed conditions rich with oxygen, filling the space left empty by mass extinctions. But their bodies overwhelmed their surroundings. It is interesting that because they were so large—too large—they became vulnerable to the slightest changes in the world. Among the animals that died out were the largest of the dinosaurs, the Brachiosauridae family, and the *Tyrannosaurus*. Dinosaurs once ruled the Earth, but their powerful size couldn't save them in the end.

As it turned out, however, the dinosaurs did not completely disappear. Thanks to recent studies, it has become clear that many dinosaurs had feathers. It seems quite possible, surprisingly, that the dinosaurs that made it through the mass extinction evolved into birds.

The dinosaurs were not the only creatures to disappear from the Earth 65 million years ago. The ammonites and many other life forms joined them. After this event, the Earth gradually began to look like it does today. And at long last, the mammals and the birds became the principal players in the game of life.

The Cenozoic Era: Age of Mammals and Primates

The Earth then entered the Cenozoic Era, the era we live in today. From the long view

3 From Dinosaur to Human

of history, the Cenozoic Era covers less than 1/70 th of the Earth's past. For example, the period between the time that the dinosaurs disappeared and the building of the Tokyo Skytree lasted fewer years than the Cretaceous Period in the Mesozoic Era alone.

Of course, to human eyes, the changes that occurred in the last 65 million years are striking when compared to what came before. However, it may be more reasonable to view the Cenozoic Era as nothing more than an extra period in the Earth's long history, following the Precambrian, the Paleozoic, and the Mesozoic eras.

We know more about the Cenozoic Era we live in than any other age. But even the history of human evolution is full of puzzles. And the further we go back in time, the deeper the shadows of ignorance grow. To strip back the layers of the history of the Earth means, in effect, to see how far human knowledge can extend into the past.

The Cenozoic Era is divided into the Paleogene, the Neocene, and the Quaternary

Periods, and each of these can be divided into even smaller periods.

In the Cenozoic Era, the continents that originated as Pangaea continued to break apart. By 20 million years ago the South American, Australian, and Antarctic continents had drifted apart, and the Indian continent, which had broken off from Africa, collided with the Eurasian continent. (By the way, the Isthmus of Panama, which connects North and South America, formed about 3.5 million years ago.) Plants and animals were both influenced by the movement of the continents as we can see from the way they changed and spread across the world.

The Earth gradually cooled during most of the Cenozoic Era, except for a brief period of warming 55 million years ago. That part of the Quaternary Period, called the Diluvium Epoch, was a time of alternating glacial and interglacial periods. The last glacial period came to an end about 10,000 years ago, marking the end of the Diluvium Epoch and the beginning of our current Holocene (Alluvial)

3 From Dinosaur to Human

Epoch. How will this period of cooling turn out? What effect will human civilization have on the environment? This is the question that humans must consider.

The most important event in the Cenozoic Era is the evolution of the mammals.

The term K-T boundary is the line dividing the Mesozoic and Cenozoic Eras, the time of the last mass extinction. Like the P-T boundary mentioned earlier, the K-T boundary indicates a period of great change. As we know, many animals became extinct, such as dinosaurs, reptilian birds, and many life forms in the ocean, including the reptile ichthyosaur. Mammals and other life forms began to fill the gaps left by this extinction.

The space left empty by the extinction of a certain life form is called a niche. The event marking the K-T boundary—the niche left by the extinction of dinosaurs and other natural enemies—was filled by the mammals. In the process, many evolutionary changes occurred as animals adapted to new living conditions. A greater variety of mammals appeared.

As the Cretaceous Period came to an end, the first animal to fill the niche and to assume the position at the top of the food chain was the *Diatryma*, a "terror bird" two meters tall that had lived through the meteor impact. The *Diatryma* were carnivorous. Most mammals, which were now little larger than a rat, tried to avoid them by hiding in trees during the day and eating fruit. The habit of eating fruit led mammals to develop a stronger grip. Some of them took to eating the eggs of the terror bird, in effect issuing a challenge for power.

Most of these terror birds gradually either became extinct or evolved into birds that are more like the birds we see today. In order to accomplish this evolution, their front legs had to turn into wings, and their body weight had to become lighter to enable flight. The birds gradually lost their leg strength and their powerful jaws for catching prey.

About 55 million years ago, just as the natural enemies of mammals were dying out, the Earth's crust moved again. Magma erupted onto the Earth's surface, breaking through layers containing the remains of ancient life forms and releasing huge amounts of methane. This event immediately brought about the beginning of global warming.

The rise in temperature led to a sudden change in plant life. Trees with broad leaves grew tall and forests formed. These forests had leaves and branches long enough to provide cover, allowing animals to move freely from one tree to another. This development made it possible for mammals to gather food without worrying about becoming prey themselves.

Better Late Than Never: The Earth Gives Birth to Humans

Examining eye structure and sight is an important tool in classifying the various roots of mammals. The eyes of early mammals, which originally were active at night, had worsened considerably when compared to the birds.

However, when mammals came to fill the niche left by the phorusrhacids ("terror birds"), the structure of their eyes underwent numerous

The History of the Earth

evolutionary changes.

Not too long ago, some very important fossils were discovered. These fossils, dating about 55 million years old, once belonged to an animal called *Shoshonius*. Fossils show that the eyes of the *Shoshonius* lined up side by side and faced forward.

Many mammals' eyes are on either side of the head. They cannot see objects in three dimensions. Because of the location of its eyes, the *Shoshonius* could see in 3D, enabling it to move more surely from tree to tree. The *Shoshonius* is our earliest, direct primate ancestor.

Other interesting animals developed at this time, too, including the animal that would in time become the elephant, and small *Miacis*, an ancestor to cats and dogs. And some mammals returned to the sea. It was at about this time that the ancestor to the whales and dolphins, the amphibious *Pakicetus*, appeared.

Pakicetus

3 From Dinosaur to Human

Later, as the Earth cooled further, the forests narrowed, and the plains spread, primates' eyes improved. They developed better sight in order to live in these changed conditions. The ability to see different colors allowed them to choose the youngest tree leaves to eat. This brought about a huge improvement in their lives. Another important change was that the evolution of the eyes gave expression to the face, which allowed for better communication.

Some primates learned to walk on two legs, which helped to steady the brain. This development also marked the beginning of their evolution to the direct ancestor of human beings, the *Pithecanthropus*. The fossils of an ancient human walking on two legs, *Ardipithecus*, were discovered in Ethiopia. They are 6 million years old. Further evolution produced the *Australopithecus*. And later, humans with more developed brains learned to make fire. These *Homo habilis*, who were active about 2 million years ago, were the first to use stones and other objects as tools.

As these human ancestors moved from

their place of birth in Africa to spread across the Eurasian continent, they evolved into *Homo erectus*, which is known to many people as the Peking man or the Java man. They later evolved into *Homo sapiens*, the human species.

Homo habilis

Modern humans have had various relatives in history. The most well known are the Neanderthal. Until recently, they were thought to be our direct ancestors. But a study of their DNA showed that the Neanderthal became extinct about 30,000 years ago.

At the very last minute in the long, magnificent history of the Earth, human beings finally had taken a huge evolutionary step forward.

Where Might We Go From Here?

From the beginning of the Earth 4.6 billion years ago to the present day, it has been a

3 From Dinosaur to Human

long, difficult journey. What, then, is to be the future of the Earth?

Up to this point, we have looked at the various changes on Earth as a record of past events. In truth, human beings are nothing but a leaf floating between a past without end and a future without bounds. Our outlook is limited by the fact that we can only see ourselves as a part of the past.

However, by understanding what we can of the past, we can make discoveries that enable us to guess the future. We can guess that the Earth will continue to repeat the same natural processes, will gradually grow old, and in the end will die along with the extinction of the sun.

Some scientists have recently argued that before that stage, we will reach a point at which human beings will no longer evolve. The principal difference between human beings and other animals is that humans have the power to observe, consider, and make judgments. More than 10,000 years have now passed since people began creating societies. In the process, humans learned not to adapt to their environment, but to artificially change their surroundings to fit their needs and desires.

First, with the use of weapons and tools, humans learned to hunt in an organized manner. Next they designed clothing and homes that would protect them from heat and cold, wind and rain. Now they are attempting to make use of every possible advance in technology to protect themselves further.

Two things should not be forgotten. First, evolution occurs when life forms are threatened by difficult conditions. Second, just as with the dinosaurs that adapted too well, life forms that grow too comfortable can be wiped out in a second when the Earth undergoes changes to which they cannot adapt.

Having gained the ability to control their environment, humans may lose the ability to adapt to difficult conditions. If humans get too used to a life of ease, our immune system might weaken and we might be left helpless when the Earth undergoes another major change.

3 From Dinosaur to Human

From the long history of the Earth, we know that it will be visited again by some terrible event—a huge volcanic explosion, a meteor impact, another Snowball Earth.

Or it may be that by changing the environment with our own culture, humans will bring about terrible changes. Remember, it was the activity of the blue-green algae that led to the Earth freezing over.

The changes brought on by human activity may amount to nothing more than a second in Earth terms. We shouldn't forget, however, that it was just such quick moments that repeatedly drove countless life forms into mass extinction.

Studying the history of the Earth, we can see that our responsibility is great.

Man Is a Thinking Reed

Thinking About the Universe

One of Paul Gauguin's famous paintings contains the words, "Where do we come from? What are we? Where are we going?" Completed in 1898, it is now displayed at the Museum of Fine Arts in Boston. We were born on Earth, are now living on Earth, and after death, we will be buried on Earth.

Of course, the universe gave birth to the Earth, the Earth gave birth to us, and the Earth will at some point oversee our death. A child of the sun, the Earth makes one revolution every 365 days at a speed of 29.78 km per second. That is 88 times faster than the standard speed of sound in the atmosphere. In concluding this book, we must examine the relationship between the Earth and the universe, and consider how we have tried to understand them both. This will lead us back to Gauguin's questions.

Human beings possess the idea of time, which lies at the center of common human knowledge. For example, we carry out our

4 Man Is a Thinking Reed

daily activities according to day and night, which even influences the rhythms of our bodies.

The speed at which we move from one point to another is measured in terms of time. The same holds true for the length of our lives. We also use time to try to understand the universe and the distance to the stars.

For example, the mean distance from the Earth to the sun is 149,597,870 km. If we should board an airplane headed for the sun traveling at 1,000 km per hour, it would take 149,597.87 hours to arrive. Because there are 24 hours in a day, if we divide this number by 24, the result is about 6,233 days. This means it would take 17 years to reach the sun. (Naturally, this couldn't actually happen because no airplane can break away from the gravity of the Earth.)

Another way to look at time is to compare the age of the Earth to the history of human beings. Let's consider the history of the Earth in terms of a human life. To make things easy, say that humans live for 100 years and the

Earth is now 50 years old. Since the Earth is now 4.6 billion years old, one human year would equal 92 million years. Divide this by 365, and one day becomes 252,000 years. As we mentioned in Chapter 3, humans got their start about 2 million years ago. Divide 2 million by 252,000 years, and the result is 7.93 days. So, if you think of the Earth's history as being equal to a person's life, for a person who is 50 years old, humans came into existence only one week ago.

Is the Earth Alone in the Universe?

The sun is one of the fixed stars. A "fixed star" is one that shines under its own power. Let us think for a moment about our system of stars, the Milky Way.

The Milky Way consists of about 200 billion fixed stars. Scientists believe that there are more than 200 billion galaxies in the universe. This means that the universe has a huge number of fixed stars, and around each star can be found planets like the Earth.

4 Man Is a Thinking Reed

Science fiction novels and movies often tell stories of aliens coming to Earth. Let's consider whether it is actually possible for such beings to have evolved. In this vast universe, is it true that humans exist only on this one lonely planet? This is an interesting question.

Remember that early man came into being 500,000 years ago, a tiny amount of time in universal terms.

Let's say you have a time machine and you can go back 500,000 years and visit our ancestors who were just a step above the monkeys. Let us say you come prepared, with a modern car, weapons, and medicine. You would be greeted as a god. Actually, there would probably be no need to go back as far as 500,000 years. A trip to ancient Egypt would produce the same results.

In what amounts to just a quick moment in universal time, living things have managed to evolve this far. So it shouldn't be surprising if there are living creatures somewhere in the universe with a civilization beyond our understanding.

Say that this alien life came into being several tens of thousands of years before humans, went through the same evolutionary process, and discovered a way to move through space at a speed faster than light. This would make the world of science fiction a reality.

Because of the huge number of stars in the universe, it wouldn't be strange if one of their planets harbored life.

Science and Gods: The Universe Becomes One

Although we have made magnificent advances in science, humans still occupy only a small and uncertain position in just one tiny corner of the universe. It is believed that since ancient times, people have created stories about the universe in order to explain it.

In even the earliest days of existence, humans most likely knew the importance of the sun. Across the world there are religions that view the sun as a god. In Japan, Amaterasu-omikami is a sun goddess.

4 Man Is a Thinking Reed

Sometimes when we try to consider our planet and the universe that stretches beyond it, we feel a fear of the unknown and shut our eyes. But by coming to know the universe that is within us, we can try to come to terms with that fear. It is probably safe to say that the Buddhist idea of enlightenment is our answer to this problem. Many religions also are based on the idea that nothing is truly unknown because a god knows all and will teach us on the other side of our lives. So we shouldn't forget that there is an approach other than science that we can use to understand the universe.

We can learn something from this. In his famous *Pensées*, the French philosopher Blaise Pascal wrote, "Man is a thinking reed." He wrote:

Man is nothing more than a feeble reed. If a wind blows, it can easily break and meet [its] death. From the perspective of the universe, what is only a slight [tremble] can bring about [the end of our world]. But [humanity] is aware of its position among the workings of the universe, and even as it is crushed to death, it can reflect on the situation it has placed itself in.

In the face of a universe that is difficult to understand, humanity has risen to the challenge with math and science. Through the development of theories and formulas, we have tried to solve the mysteries of the universe. When one path fails to provide an answer, we try another path. This is the process of trial and error.

With trial and error, religion, and philosophy, humanity has evolved beyond eyes, ears, nose, mouth, and touch to arrive at an awareness of a new power that we can call "heart."

It is the evolution of the heart that has brought about the height of "wisdom." Is it not this last tool, the most important tool of all, that will enable human beings to live in harmony with the Earth for years to come?

Word List

- 本文で使われている全ての語を掲載しています（LEVEL 1, 2）。ただし、LEVEL 3以上は、中学校レベルの語を含みません。
- 語形が規則変化する語の見出しは原形で示しています。不規則変化語は本文中で使われている形になっています。
- 一般的な意味を紹介していますので、一部の語で本文で実際に使われている品詞や意味と合っていないことがあります。
- 品詞は以下のように示しています。

名 名詞	代 代名詞	形 形容詞	副 副詞	動 動詞	助 助動詞
前 前置詞	接 接続詞	間 間投詞	冠 冠詞	略 略語	俗 俗語
頭 接頭語	尾 接尾語	号 記号	関 関係代名詞		

A

- **abdomen** 名 腹, 腹部
- **abdominal breathing** 腹式呼吸
- **ability** 名 (～する)能力
- **absorb** 動 吸収する
- **abundant** 形 豊富な
- **accident** 名 偶然
- **accompanied by** 《be –》～と同時に起こる, ～に付随して起こる
- **accomplish** 動 成し遂げる, 果たす
- **according to** ～に従って
- **account** 名 説明, 報告, 記述
- **accumulate** 動 蓄積する, 積もる
- **acid** 形 酸性の 名 酸 amino acid アミノ酸
- **acidic** 形 酸性の
- **act** 名 行為
- **active** 形 活動的な, 盛んな
- **activity** 名 活動
- **actual** 形 実際の
- **actually** 副 実際に, 本当に
- **adapt** 動 適応する[させる]
- **adaptation** 名 順応, 適応
- **Adelobasileus** 名 アデロバシレウス《最古の哺乳類》
- **adult** 名 大人, 成人
- **advance** 名 進歩, 前進 動 前進する
- **advanced** 形 進化した, 高度な
- **affect** 動 影響する
- **Africa** 名 アフリカ《大陸》
- **again and again** 何度も繰り返して
- **age** 熟 age of ～の時代 golden age 全盛期, 黄金時代
- **ago** 熟 long ago ずっと前に, 昔
- **air sac** 空気袋, 空気嚢
- **airplane** 名 飛行機
- **Alexander Oparin** アレクサンドル・オパーリン《人名, ソ連の科学者。1894–1980》
- **algae** 名 藻(類)《algaの複数形》
- **alien** 形 ①宇宙人 ②なじみがない, 異質の
- **all** 熟 for all we know おそらく once and for all 決定的に
- **allow** 動 ①《– to》～が…するのを可能にする, ～に…させておく ②

WORD LIST

与える
- **Alluvial Epoch** 堆積期
- **along with** 〜と一緒に
- **alternate** 動 交互に起こる
- **although** 接 〜だけれども、たとえ〜でも
- **Amaterasu-omikami** 名 天照大神《日本神話の神》
- **American** 形 アメリカ(人)の
- **amino acid** アミノ酸
- **ammonia** 名 アンモニア
- **ammonite** 名 アンモナイト《古代生物》
- **amount** 名 ①量、額 ②《the -》合計 動 結局〜になる
- **amphibian** 名 両生類
- **amphibious** 形 水陸両生の
- **ancestor** 名 祖先、先祖
- **ancestral** 形 祖先の、先祖代々の
- **ancient** 形 古代の
- **and so on** 〜など、その他もろもろ
- **anger** 名 怒り
- **another** 熟 one another お互い
- **anoxic** 形 無酸素の oceanic anoxic event 海洋無酸素事変
- **Antarctic** 形 南極(地方)の
- **Antarctica** 名 南極
- **any** 熟 than any other ほかのどの〜よりも
- **anywhere** 副 どこにも
- **apart** 副 ばらばらに、離れて tear apart 引き裂く、ばらばらにする
- **appear** 動 現れる、見えてくる
- **appearance** 名 現れること、出現
- **apply** 動 あてはまる
- **approach** 動 接近する 名 (〜へ)近づく道
- **Archaeopteryx** 名 始祖鳥《古代生物》
- **Archean Era** 始生代
- **archosaur** 名 祖竜《古代生物》
- **Arctic** 形 北極の
- **Ardipithecus** アルディピテクス属《原始人類》
- **argue** 動 論じる、議論する
- **arthropod** 名 節足動物
- **artificially** 副 人工的に
- **as** 熟 as far as 〜まで、〜する限り(では) as long as 〜する以上は、〜である限りは as well as 〜と同様に just as 〜と全く同じように、〜と同じくらいに such as たとえば〜、〜のような
- **ash** 名 灰
- **Asia** 名 アジア
- **Asian** 形 アジアの
- **assume** 動 (地位などに)就く
- **astronomer** 名 天文学者
- **at** 熟 at one time かつては at that time その時 at the time そのころ、当時は at the time of 〜の際に at this time このとき
- **athlete's heart** スポーツ心臓
- **atm** 略 気圧《= atmosphere》
- **atmosphere** 名 ①大気、空気 ②気圧
- **atmospheric** 形 大気の
- **atom** 名 原子
- **attach** 動 付着する
- **attack** 動 襲う
- **attempt** 動 〜しようとする、〜を企てる
- **attention** 名 注意
- **attract** 動 引きつける
- **aurora** 名 オーロラ
- **Australia** 名 オーストラリア《国名》
- **Australian** 形 オーストラリアの
- **Australopithecus** 名 アウスト

The History of the Earth

ラロピテクス属《原始人類》
- **available** 形 得られる
- **avoid** 動 避ける
- **aware of** 《be –》～に気がついている
- **awareness** 名 認識, 自覚

B

- **balance** 名 均衡
- **barely** 副 かろうじて
- **basalt** 名 玄武岩
- **based on** 《be –》～に基づく
- **basic** 形 基本の
- **battle** 名 戦い
- **bay** 名 湾, 入り江
- **beaker** 名 ビーカー
- **bear** 動 耐える
- **beat** 動 打ち負かす, やっつける beat up ひどい目に遭わす
- **because of** ～のために, ～の理由で
- **beginning** 名 初め, 始まり
- **being** 名 存在, 生命, 人間 come into being 生じる, 発生する human being 人, 人間
- **belong to** ～に属する
- **below** 前 ①～より下に ②～以下の 副 下に[へ]
- **beneath** 前 ～の下に[の]
- **between A and B** AとBの間に
- **beyond** 前 ～を越えて, ～の向こうに 副 向こうに
- **Big Bang** ビッグバン《宇宙創生の大爆発》
- **Big Crunch** ビッグクランチ《予測される宇宙終焉時の大収縮》
- **billion** 名 10億 形 ばく大な, 無数の
- **biota** 名 生物相
- **birth** 名 ①出産, 誕生 ②生まれ, 起源 give birth 出産する give birth to ～を生む
- **Blaise Pascal** ブレーズ・パスカル《人名, フランスの学者。1623–1662》
- **block** 熟 building blocks of life 生物の構成単位
- **blow** 動 (風が)吹く, (風が)～を吹き飛ばす 名 打撃 blow apart ～をばらばらに吹き飛ばす
- **blown** 動 blow (吹く)の過去分詞
- **blue-green algae** 藍藻類
- **board** 動 乗り込む
- **bombardment** 名 衝撃, 爆撃
- **bone** 名 骨,《-s》骨格
- **Boston** 名 ボストン《地名》
- **both A and B** AもBも
- **bottom** 名 底, 最下位
- **bound** 名 限度 without bound 際限なく
- **boundary** 名 境界線
- **Brachiosauridae** 名 ブラキオサウルス《恐竜》
- **brain** 名 脳
- **branch** 名 枝
- **break into** ～に食い込む
- **break through** ～を突き破る
- **break up** ばらばらになる, 解散させる
- **breathe** 動 呼吸する
- **breathing** 名 呼吸 abdominal breathing 腹式呼吸
- **brief** 形 短い時間の
- **bring about** 引き起こす
- **bring up** 育てる
- **broad** 形 幅の広い
- **Buddhist** 形 仏教の, 仏陀の
- **building** 名 建物, ビル building

Word List

- blocks of life 生物の構成単位
- **Burgess Shale** バージェス頁岩
- **burst** 名爆発
- **bury** 動覆い隠す,埋める
- **but** 熟 not ~ but ~ではなくて… nothing but ~にすぎない
- **by the way** ところで,ついでに

C

- **calm** 動落ち着かせる
- **Cambrian Period** カンブリア紀
- **Canadian Rockies** カナディアン・ロッキー《地名》
- **cancer** 名癌
- **carbide** 名炭化物
- **carbon** 名炭素 carbon dioxide 二酸化炭素
- **Carboniferous Period** 石炭紀
- **carbonize** 動炭化する
- **carnivore** 名肉食動物
- **carnivorous** 形肉食(性)の
- **carry back** (元に)戻す
- **carry out** 実施する,実行する
- **cartilaginous** 形軟骨質の
- **carve** 動彫る
- **catch a cold** 風邪を引く
- **cattle** 名家畜
- **celestial body** 天体
- **cell** 名細胞
- **cellular** 形細胞の
- **Celsius** 名セ氏
- **Cenozoic Era** 新生代
- **centimeter** 名センチメートル《長さの単位》1 square centimeter 一センチ平方
- **central** 形中心の,主要な
- **certain** 形①確実な ②ある,いくらかの
- **CH₄** 名メタン
- **challenge** 名試練,難関 issue a challenge 挑戦する
- **chapter** 名(書物の)章
- **charge** 名負荷 electrical charge 電荷
- **chemical** 形化学的な
- **chest** 名胸,肺
- **Chicxulub Crater** チクシュルーブ・クレーター《小惑星衝突跡》
- **childhood** 名幼年[子ども]時代
- **China** 名中国《国名》
- **Chinese** 名中国人
- **choanocyte** 名襟細胞
- **choanoflagellate** 名襟鞭毛虫《微生物》
- **chromosome** 名染色体
- **circle** 動(~の周囲を)回る
- **circulate** 動流れる
- **circumstance** 名環境
- **civilization** 名文明
- **classification** 名分類,区分
- **classify** 動分類する
- **clear** 形はっきりした,明白な
- **clearly** 副はっきりと
- **clever** 形利口な
- **climate** 名気候
- **clock** 熟 turn the clock back 時計を巻き戻す
- **close** 熟 take a closer look より詳しく見る
- **closely** 副密接に
- **clothing** 名衣類
- **CO₂** 名二酸化炭素
- **coal** 名石炭,木炭
- **Coelophysis** 名コエロフィシス《恐竜》
- **cold** 熟 catch a cold 風邪を引く

The History of the Earth

- **collagen** 名コラーゲン
- **collide** 動ぶつかる, 衝突する
- **collision** 名衝突
- **color** 動変色する
- **Columbia** 名コロンビア《地名》
- **combine** 動結合する[させる]
- **come** 熟 come after ～のあとを追う come back to ～へ帰ってくる, ～に戻る come into being 生じる, 発生する come into existence 出現する, 誕生する come to mind 思い浮かぶ come to terms with ～と折り合いを付ける
- **comfortable** 形快適な
- **common** 熟 have something in common 共通点がある
- **communicate** 動交信する
- **communication** 名情報の伝達, コミュニケーション
- **compare** 動①比較する ②たとえる be compared to ～と比較して
- **complete** 形完全な, まったくの 動完成させる
- **completely** 副完全に, すっかり
- **complex** 形複雑な, 複合体の
- **compound** 名化合物
- **concern** 動関係する
- **conclude** 動①終える ②結論を下す
- **condition** 名①(健康)状態, 境遇 ②《-s》状況 ③条件
- **conduct** 動伝導する
- **conifer** 名針葉樹
- **connect** 動つながる, つなぐ
- **connection** 名つながり, 関係
- **consider** 動①熟考する, 考慮する ②(～と)みなす ③気にかける, 思いやる
- **considerable** 形相当な, かなりの
- **considerably** 副かなり, 相当に
- **consist of** (部分・要素から)成る
- **constant** 形一定の
- **contain** 動含む, 入っている
- **content** 名《-s》目次
- **continent** 名大陸, 陸地
- **continental shelves** 大陸棚
- **continually** 副継続的に, 絶えず
- **contract** 動縮小する
- **contraction** 名収縮
- **control** 動管理[支配]する 名管理, 支配
- **convection** 名対流, 上昇気流
- **convert** 動変える, 変わる
- **cool down** 冷える
- **copy** 動複製する, コピーする
- **core** 名核心, 中心
- **cosmic ray** 宇宙線
- **could have done** ～だったかもしれない《仮定法》
- **countercurrent** 名逆流
- **countless** 形無数の
- **course** 熟 of course もちろん, 当然
- **cover** 動①覆う, 包む ②(～に)わたる, 及ぶ 名やぶ, 下生え
- **covering** 名覆い, 被膜
- **crack** 名割れ目, ひび
- **crash into** ～と衝突する
- **crater** 名隕石孔, クレーター
- **create** 動創造する, 生み出す
- **creation** 名創造[物]
- **creature** 名(神の)創造物, 生物
- **Cretaceous Period** 白亜紀
- **crocodile** 名ワニ類
- **cruel** 形過酷な, 厳しい
- **crunch** 動踏み潰すこと Big Crunch ビッグクランチ, 宇宙大収縮

Word List

- **crushed to death** 《be –》激突死する
- **crust** 名 堅い表面, 地殻
- **current** 形 現在の 名 流れ, 電流
- **currently** 副 今のところ, 現在
- **cut off** 断ち切る, 遮断する
- **cyanobacteria** 名 藍色細菌, シアノバクテリア
- **cycle** 動 ~を循環させる
- **cynodont** 名 キノドン類《古代生物》

D

- **daily** 形 毎日の, 日常の
- **damage** 動 損害を与える
- **day** 熟 day and night 昼も夜も one day (過去の)ある日, (未来の)いつか
- **deal** 名 (不特定の)量, 額 a great deal of 多量の, 大量の
- **death** 名 ①死 ②《the –》終焉, 消滅 be crushed to death 激突死する death sentence 死刑宣告
- **decline** 動 減少する, 低下する 名 減少
- **defeat** 名 敗北
- **deflate** 動 収縮する
- **degree** 名 (温度・角度の) 度
- **dense** 形 濃い, 密集した
- **density** 名 濃度
- **depend on** ~に頼る
- **depth** 名 深さ
- **descend into** 動 ~へ下降する
- **descendant** 名 子孫, 末えい
- **describe** 動 特徴づける
- **deserve** 動 (~して)当然である
- **design** 動 ~を考案する
- **desire** 名 欲求
- **destabilize** 動 ~を不安定にする
- **destroy** 動 破壊する, 絶滅させる
- **develop** 動 発達する[させる]
- **development** 名 発達, 進歩
- **Devonian Period** デボン紀
- **diameter** 名 直径
- **diaphragm** 名 横隔膜
- **Diatryma** 名 ディアトリマ《古代生物》
- **die out** 絶滅する
- **digestive** 形 消化の
- **Diluvium Epoch** 洪積世
- **dimension** 名 次元
- **dinosaur** 名 恐竜
- **dioxide** 名 二酸化物 carbon dioxide 二酸化炭素
- **direct** 形 直接の
- **direction** 名 方向
- **directly** 副 ①じかに ②まっすぐに ③ちょうど
- **disappear** 動 姿を消す, なくなる
- **discovery** 名 発見
- **discuss** 動 議論[検討]する
- **disinfectant** 名 殺菌[消毒]剤
- **display** 動 展示する 名 展示
- **distance** 名 距離, 隔たり
- **distant** 形 遠い, 隔たった
- **divide** 動 分かれる, 分ける be divided into 分けられる, 分類される
- **division** 名 分裂
- **DNA** 略 デオキシリボ核酸《= deoxyribonucleic acid》
- **do well** 栄える
- **dolphin** 名 イルカ
- **doubt** 熟 no doubt きっと, たぶん
- **down there** 下の方で[に]
- **draw** 動 引く, 引っ張る

The History of the Earth

- **drawn** 動 draw（引く）の過去分詞
- **drew** 動 draw（引く）の過去
- **drift apart** だんだん離れていく
- **drive** 動 ～に追いやる, 推進する
- **driving force** 原動力
- **drove** 動 drive（追いやる）の過去
- **due to** ～によって, ～が原因で
- **dull** 形 くすんだ, 味気ない
- **Dunkleosteus** 名 ダンクレオステウス《古代生物》
- **dust** 名 ちり, ほこり
- **dying** 動 die（死ぬ）の現在分詞

E

- **each other** お互いに
- **earth** 熟 in the earth 地中に
- **earthquake** 名 地震, 大変動
- **ease** 名 安心
- **easily** 副 容易に, たやすく
- **echinoderm** 名 棘皮動物
- **ecosystem** 名 生態系
- **edge** 名 へり, 端, 境界
- **Ediacara** エディアカラ《地名》 Ediacara biota エディアカラ生物群
- **Edwin Hubble** エドウィン・ハッブル《人名》
- **effect** 名 影響, 効果 in effect 実際には, 事実上
- **efficiency** 名 効率
- **efficient** 形 効率的な
- **efficiently** 副 効果的に
- **Egypt** 名 エジプト《国名》
- **either** 熟 either A or B AかそれともB either side of ～の両側に on either side 両側に
- **electric** 形 電気の
- **electrical charge** 電荷

- **electricity** 名 電気
- **electromagnetic** 形 電磁気の
- **element** 名 成分, 元素
- **embryo** 名 胚
- **enable** 動 （～することを）可能にする
- **encourage** 動 促進する
- **end** 熟 at the end of ～の終わりに in the end とうとう, 結局
- **endanger** 動 ～を危険にさらす
- **endure** 動 耐え忍ぶ, 持ちこたえる
- **enemy** 名 敵
- **energize** 動 ～を活性化する
- **engrave** 動 刻む
- **enlightenment** 名 悟り
- **enough to do** ～するのに十分な
- **entire** 形 全体の
- **entirely** 副 完全に, まったく
- **environment** 名 環境
- **epoch** 名 世《地質学の時代単位》
- **equal** 形 等しい 動 匹敵する, 等しい be equal to ～に等しい
- **equator** 名《the –》赤道
- **era** 名 時代, 年代
- **error** 名 間違い, 過失
- **erupt** 動 （火山が）噴火する, 噴出する
- **eruption** 名 爆発, 噴火
- **escape** 動 逃げる, 免れる
- **establish** 動 確立する
- **Ethiopia** 名 エチオピア《国名》
- **eukaryote** 名 真核生物
- **Eurasian continent** ユーラシア大陸
- **Europe** 名 ヨーロッパ
- **Eusthenopteron** 名 エウステノプテロン《古代生物》
- **evaporate** 動 蒸発する[させる]

WORD LIST

- **even if** たとえ〜でも
- **even though** 〜であるけれども, 〜にもかかわらず
- **eventually** 副 結局は
- **evidence** 名 証拠, 形跡
- **evolution** 名 進化
- **evolutionary** 形 進化の
- **evolve** 動 進化する[させる]
- **examine** 動 〜を分析[観察]する
- **example** 熟 for example たとえば
- **except for** 〜を除いて
- **exist** 動 存在する, 生存する
- **existence** 名 存在 come into existence 出現する, 誕生する
- **expand** 動 拡張[拡大]する
- **expansion** 名 拡張
- **experiment** 名 実験
- **explode** 動 爆発する
- **explosion** 名 爆発
- **explosive** 形 爆発的な
- **express** 動 述べる
- **expression** 名 表情
- **extend into** 〜に及ぶ
- **extinct** 形 消えた, 絶滅した
- **extinction** 名 絶滅, 死滅
- **extra** 形 追加の, 余分の

F

- **face** 熟 in (the) face of 〜に直面して
- **fact** 熟 in fact つまり, 実は, 要するに
- **fail** 動《- to》〜し損なう, 〜できない
- **failed** 形 機能不全の
- **fairly** 副 かなり, 相当に
- **fall back** 戻る, 後退する
- **fall into** 〜の状態になる
- **familiar** 形 おなじみの
- **far** 熟 as far as 〜まで, 〜する限り(では) how far どこまで
- **farther** 副 もっと遠く, さらに進んだ
- **fear** 名 恐れ, 不安
- **feather** 名《-s》羽毛
- **fed** 動 feed (餌を食べる) の過去, 過去分詞
- **feeble** 形 弱い, もろい
- **feed on** 〜を餌にする
- **female** 形 女性の, 雌の
- **fern** 名 シダ(羊歯)《植物》
- **fertilization** 名 受精
- **fetus** 名 胎児
- **fever** 名 熱病
- **fiber** 名 繊維, 繊維質
- **fiction** 名 小説
- **fierce** 形 すさまじい, 猛烈な
- **fig** 名 イチジク
- **fight off** 戦って撃退する, 〜に抗う
- **fin** 名 (魚などの)ひれ, ひれ状のもの
- **final** 形 最終の
- **first** 熟 for the first time 初めて
- **fit** 動 適合する, 合致させる
- **fixed** 形 一定の, 定着した fixed star 恒星
- **flagella** 名 flagellum(鞭毛)の複数
- **flagellum** 名 鞭毛
- **flame** 名 炎
- **flare** 名 爆発, ゆらめく炎
- **flash** 名 きらめき, フラッシュ
- **flask** 名 フラスコ
- **flat** 形 平らな

The History of the Earth

- **flight** 動飛ぶ
- **float** 動浮かぶ, 漂流する
- **flood** 動〜を水浸しにする
- **flow** 動流れ出る, 流れる
- **following** 形《the –》次の, 次に続く
- **for all we know** おそらく
- **for example** たとえば
- **force** 名力 動力ずくで〜する, 押しやる **driving force** 原動力
- **form** 名形, 形態, 構造 動形づくる
- **formation** 名構造, 構成
- **formula** 名化学式, 公式
- **forward** 形前方の 副①前方に ②将来に向けて
- **fossil** 名化石
- **foundation** 名基礎, 土台
- **fragment** 名破片, かけら
- **framework** 名構造
- **freely** 副自由に
- **freeze** 動凍る 名氷結 **freeze over** 氷で覆う
- **French** 形フランス(人・語)の
- **friendly** 形心地よい
- **from now** 今から, これから
- **from 〜 to** 〜から…まで
- **froze** 動freeze(凍る)の過去
- **frozen** 形凍った
- **full of** 《be –》〜で一杯である
- **function** 名機能
- **further** 形その上の, なおいっそうの 副もっと, さらに進んで
- **fusion** 名融合
- **future** 名 **in the future** 将来は

G

- **gain** 動獲得する
- **galaxy** 名銀河系, 星雲
- **gamma ray** ガンマ線
- **gap** 名すき間
- **gas** 名気体, ガス
- **gather** 動集まる, 集める
- **gene** 名遺伝子
- **generation** 名一世代
- **genetic** 形遺伝子の
- **genetically** 副遺伝子学的に
- **genetics** 名遺伝学
- **genuine** 形本物の, 純粋な
- **geological** 形地質学の
- **get to know** 知るようになる
- **Giant Impact** ジャイアント・インパクト説, 巨大衝突説
- **gigantic** 形巨大な
- **give birth** 出産する
- **give birth to** 〜を生む
- **give rise to** 〜を引き起こす
- **glacial** 形氷河期の
- **glaciation** 名氷河期
- **glance** 名一べつ **at a glance** 一目見ただけで
- **global** 形地球規模の
- **go down** 衰える, 低下する
- **go on to** 〜に取り掛かる
- **go through** 経る, 経験する
- **goddess** 名女神
- **golden age** 全盛期, 黄金時代
- **Gondwana** 名ゴンドワナ大陸《古代の大陸》
- **gradually** 副だんだんと
- **granite** 名花崗岩, 御影石
- **gravity** 名重力, 引力
- **great deal of** 《a –》多量の, 大量の
- **Great Britain** グレート・ブリテン(島)

Word List

- **greatly** 副 大いに
- **Greenland** 名 グリーンランド《地名》
- **greet** 動 (喜んで)迎える
- **grip** 名 つかむこと, 握力
- **grow to** ～に成長する
- **grow up** 成長する
- **grow up to be** 成長して～になる
- **growth** 名 成長, 発展

H

- **habit** 名 習慣
- **Hadean Era** 冥王代
- **handle** 動 処理する
- **harbor** 動 ～を内に宿す
- **harmful** 形 有害な
- **harmony** 名 調和
- **Harold Urey** ハロルド・ユーリー《人名, アメリカの化学者。1893–1981》
- **hate** 動 憎む
- **have** 熟 could have done ～だったかもしれない《仮定法》 have something in common 共通点がある
- **head for** ～に向かう
- **heat** 名 熱, 暑さ 動 熱する, 暖める
- **heaven** 名 天国
- **height** 名 ①高さ, 身長 ②《the-》絶頂, 真っ盛り at the height of ～の絶頂期で
- **helium** 名 ヘリウム
- **helpful** 形 役に立つ
- **helpless** 形 無力の, 自分ではどうすることもできない
- **herbivorous** 形 草食性の
- **here are** こちらは～です
- **hidden** 動 hide (隠れる) の過去分詞 形 隠れた
- **hide** 動 隠れる, 隠れて見えない
- **Himalayas** 名 ヒマラヤ山脈
- **historical** 形 歴史の
- **Holocene Epoch** 完新世
- **Homo erectus** ホモ・エレクトス《原始人類》
- **Homo habilis** ホモ・ハビリス《原始人類》
- **Homo sapiens** ホモ・サピエンス, 人類
- **how far** どこまで
- **how to** ～する方法
- **however** 接 けれども, だが
- **huge** 形 巨大な, ばく大な
- **human being** 人, 人間
- **humanity** 名 ①人間性 ②人類
- **humid** 形 湿度の高い
- **humidity** 名 湿気
- **hunt** 動 狩りをする
- **Huronian glaciation** ヒューロニアン氷河
- **hydrochloric acid** 塩酸
- **hydrogen** 名 水素

I

- **ichthyosaur** 名 魚竜《古代生物》
- **Ichthyostega** 名 イクチオステガ《古代生物》
- **if** 熟 even if たとえ～でも
- **ignorance** 名 知らないこと
- **illness** 名 病気
- **immediately** 副 すぐに
- **immune** 形 免疫の
- **impact** 名 衝突, 衝撃 Giant Impact ジャイアント・インパクト説, 巨大衝突説
- **importance** 名 重要性

The History of the Earth

- **impressive** 形 目覚しい, 印象的な
- **improve** 動 改善する[させる], 進歩する
- **improvement** 名 改善
- **include** 動 含む, (主語)には〜がある[挙げられる]
- **including** 前 〜を含めて, 込みで
- **increase** 動 増える, 増やす, 高まる, 拡大する[させる] 名 増大
- **India** 名 インド《国名》
- **Indian** 形 インドの
- **indicate** 動 (ものの存在などを)示す, 意味する
- **individual** 形 独立した, 個々の 名 個体, 個人
- **Indonesia** 名 インドネシア《国名》
- **inferior** 形 (質の)劣った
- **influence** 名 影響 動 影響をおよぼす
- **injury** 名 けが
- **inorganic** 形 無機の, 無生物の
- **instead** 副 その代わりに instead of 〜の代わりに
- **intake** 名 摂取
- **intense** 形 強烈な, 激しい
- **interglacial period** 間氷期
- **interior** 形 内部の
- **internal** 形 内部の
- **introduction** 名 序文
- **ion** 名 イオン
- **iridium** 名 イリジウム
- **iron** 名 鉄
- **irradiate** 動 〜に放射線[光]を当てる
- **issue a challenge** 挑戦する
- **Isthmus of Panama** パナマ海峡《地名》
- **it is 〜 for someone to** (人)が…するのは〜だ
- **it takes 〜 to** 〜の時間[労力]が必要である
- **itself** 代 それ自体, それ自身

J

- **Japan** 名 日本《国名》
- **Japanese** 名 日本人
- **Java man** ジャワ原人《原始人類》
- **jaw** 名 あご
- **journey** 名 (遠い目的地への)旅
- **judgment** 名 判断
- **Jupiter** 名 木星
- **Jurassic Period** ジュラ紀
- **just as** 〜と全く同じように, 〜と同じくらいに

K

- **keep out of** 〜を避ける
- **keep someone from** 〜から(人)を阻む
- **kilometer** 名 キロメートル《長さの単位》
- **kind of** 〜のようなもの
- **kingdom** 名 王国, 〜界
- **km** 名 キロメートル《単位》
- **know** 熟 be known as 〜として知られている be known to 〜に知られている for all we know おそらく get to know 知るようになる know of 〜について知っている
- **knowledge** 名 知識, 理解
- **K-T boundary** K-T境界

L

- **lack** 名 不足, 欠乏

Word List

- **land mass** 大陸
- **largely** 副 大規模に
- **large-scale** 形 大規模の
- **last** 熟 at long last やっとのことで
- **later** 熟 sooner or later 遅かれ早かれ
- **lateral** 形 横に向かった
- **Latin** 形 ラテン(語・系)の
- **latter half of** ～の後半
- **Laurasia** ローラシア大陸《太古の大陸》
- **lava** 名 溶岩
- **lay** 動 ①卵を産む ②lie(位置する)の過去
- **layer** 名 層,地層,積み重ね
- **lead to** ～を引き起こす,～に至る,～に通じる
- **learner** 名 学習者
- **least** 熟 at least 少なくとも
- **led** 動 lead(導く)の過去,過去分詞
- **length** 名 長さ,たけ
- **less than** ～に満たない,～未満の
- **let loose** 解き放つ,爆発させる
- **let us say** 例えば
- **level** 名 ①(高さの)基準位置 ②水準,度合い ③段階,地位 sea level 海水位
- **lie** 動 (ものごとがある領域に)位置する,ある
- **life** 熟 building blocks of life 生物の構成単位 way of life 暮らし方
- **lightning** 名 雷,稲妻
- **like** 熟 look like ～に似ている be shaped like ～のような形をしている
- **likely** 形 ありそうな,(～)しそうな 副 たぶん,おそらく
- **lily** 名 ユリ sea lily ウミユリ《棘皮動物》
- **limit** 名 限界 動 制限[限定]する
- **liquid** 名 液体 形 液体(状)の
- **lit** 動 light(火をつける)の過去,過去分詞
- **live on** 生き続ける
- **live through** (危機などを)乗り越える
- **liverwort** 名 コケ類
- **living** 名 生活 形 生きている,現存の
- **location** 名 位置,場所
- **lonely** 形 孤独な
- **long** 熟 as long as ～する以上は,～である限りは at long last やっとのことで long ago ずっと前に,昔 no longer もはや～でない[～しない]
- **look** 熟 look ahead 先[将来]を見越す look like ～に似ている take a closer look より詳しく見る take a look at ～をちょっと見る
- **loose** 形 自由な,(結びつきが)外れた let loose 解き放つ,爆発させる set loose 放つ
- **lord** 名 主人
- **loving** 形 愛情あふれる
- **lower** 形 もっと低い,下級の
- **lung** 名 肺
- **lying** 動 lie(横たわる)の現在分詞

M

- **magma** 名 溶岩,マグマ
- **magnetic** 形 磁気の
- **magnetism** 名 磁力,磁気
- **magnificent** 形 壮大な,すばらしい
- **magnitude** 名 マグニチュード《単位》
- **major** 形 大規模な,深刻な 動 専攻する
- **make** 熟 be made of ～でできて

The History of the Earth

[作られて]いる be made up of 〜で構成されている make it possible for 〜 to 〜が…できるようにする make one's way 進む, 行く make up 作り出す, 〜を形成する make use of 〜を利用する, 〜を生かす
- male 名 男性, 雄
- mammal 名 哺乳動物
- mammal-like reptile 哺乳類型爬虫類《古代生物》
- manage 動 うまく処理する, どうにか〜する
- manner 名 方法, やり方
- mantle 名 地殻, マントル
- Marchantiophyta 名 コケ類
- Marinoan glaciation マリノア氷河期
- mark 動 (事の起こりなどを)示す, 跡を残す
- Mars 名 火星
- mass 名 ①塊, (密集した)集まり ②多数, 多量 形 大量の, 大規模な land mass 大陸
- material 名 材料, 原料
- matter 熟 a matter of 〜の問題 not matter 問題にならない
- meaning 名 意味
- means of 〜する手段
- measure 動 測る, (〜の)寸法がある
- Mediterranean 名《the -》地中海
- melt 動 溶ける
- mention 動 (〜について)述べる, 言及する
- Mercury 名 水星
- Mesozoic Era 中生代
- metal 名 金属
- metallic 形 金属の
- metazoan 名 後生動物
- meteor 名 流星, 隕石
- meter 名 メートル《長さの単位》
- methane 名 メタン
- Miacis 名 ミアキス《古代生物》
- microorganism 名 微生物
- middle 名 最中
- might 助《mayの過去》①〜かもしれない ②〜してもよい, 〜できる
- Milky Way 天の川
- Miller-Urey experiment ユーリー・ミラーの実験
- mind 名 心 come to mind 思い浮かぶ
- mineral 名 無機物, 鉱物
- mission 名 使命, 伝道
- modern 形 現代[近代]の
- molecular 形 分子の
- molecule 名 分子, 微粒子
- mollusk 名 軟体動物
- molten 形 (熱で)溶かされた
- moment 名 瞬間, ちょっとの間 for a moment 少しの間
- monkey 名 サル(猿)
- monoxide 名 一酸化物 carbon monoxide 一酸化炭素
- more 熟 more and more ますます more than 〜以上 once more もう一度
- mostly 副 主として, 多くは, ほとんど
- move away from 〜から遠ざかる
- move on どんどん進む
- movement 名 動き, 運動, 変動
- multicellular 多細胞の
- multiply 動 数が増える, 繁殖する
- **Museum of Fine Arts in Boston** ボストン美術館
- mushroom 名 ①キノコ ②キノコ状のもの
- mutation 名 突然変異(種)

WORD LIST

- mystery 名 神秘, 不可思議

N

- narrow 動 狭くなる[する]
- Nasu Highlands 那須高原《地名》
- naturally 副 自然に, 当然
- nautilus 名 オウムガイ《軟体動物》
- Neanderthal 名 ネアンデルタール《原始人類》
- nearly 副 ほとんど, 大体
- necessary 形 必要な, 必須の
- need to do ～する必要がある
- Neocene 名 新第三紀
- Neptune 名 海王星
- nerve 名 神経
- network 名 網状組織, ネットワーク
- news 名 知らせ, ニュース
- niche 名 生態的地位
- night 熟 day and night 昼も夜も
- nitrogen 名 窒素
- no doubt きっと, たぶん
- no longer もはや～でない[～しない]
- no one 誰も[一人も]～ない
- normally 副 普通は, 通常は
- North America 北アメリカ, 北米
- northern 形 北の
- not matter 問題にならない
- not yet まだ～してない
- not ～ but ～ではなくて…
- note 名 注釈, 注意 動 注意[注目]する
- nothing but ～にすぎない
- novel 名 (長編)小説
- now 熟 from now 今から, これから now that 今や～だから, ～からには
- nuclear 形 原子核の nuclear fusion 核融合
- nucleus 名 細胞核
- number of 《a－》いくつかの～, 多くの～
- numerous 形 多数の
- Nuna 名 ヌーナ大陸《太古の大陸》
- nutrient 名 栄養素
- nutrition 名 栄養(物)

O

- object 名 物, 物体
- observe 動 観察[観測]する
- occupy 動 占領する
- occur 動 (事が)起こる, 生じる, (考えなどが)浮かぶ
- oceanic 形 大洋の oceanic anoxic event 海洋無酸素事変
- odds 名 勝算 against all odds 大きな困難にも関わらず
- of course もちろん, 当然
- offer 動 提案する
- on 熟 and so on ～など, その他もろもろ on the move 活発で
- once and for all 決定的に
- once more もう一度
- one 熟 at one time かつては no one 誰も[一人も]～ない one another お互い one day (過去の)ある日, (未来の)いつか one of ～の1つ[人]
- onto 前 ～の上へ[に]
- or so ～かそこらで
- or so it is said そのように言われているが
- orbit 名 軌道

The History of the Earth

- **order** 熟 in order for someone to (人)が〜するために in order to 〜するために, 〜しようと
- **ordinary** 形 普通の, 通常の
- **Ordovician Period** オルドビス紀
- **organ** 名 (体の)器官, 組織
- **organic** 形 有機(体)の
- **organism** 名 有機体, 生物
- **organized** 形 組織化された
- **origin** 名 起源, 出自 The Origin of Life『生命の起源』《著作》
- **originally** 副 元は
- **originate** 動 由来する, 起源がある
- **Orion Arm** オリオン渦状腕《銀河》
- **other** 熟 each other お互いに in other words すなわち, 言い換えれば than any other ほかのどの〜よりも
- **outer** 形 外側の
- **outlook** 名 見解
- **outward** 副 外側へ
- **overcome** 動 克服する
- **oversee** 動 注意深く見守る
- **overview** 名 大要, あらまし
- **overwhelm** 動 力で圧倒する, 打ちのめす
- **own** 熟 on one's own 自力で
- **oxidize** 動 酸化させる
- **oxygen** 名 酸素
- **ozone** 名 オゾン

P

- **painting** 名 絵画
- **Pakicetus** 名 パキケトゥス《古代生物》
- **Paleogene** 名 古第三紀
- **Paleozoic Era** 古生代
- **palm** 名 ヤシ
- **Panama** 名 パナマ《国名》
- **Pangaea** 名 パンゲア大陸《太古の大陸》
- **Pannotia** 名 パノティア大陸《太古の大陸》
- **Panthalassa** 名 パンサラッサ大洋《パンゲア大陸を囲う大洋》
- **paradise** 名 地上の楽園
- **parent** 名《-s》両親
- **part** 熟 play a part 役目を果たす
- **particle** 名 粒子
- **particular** 形 特別の in particular 特に, とりわけ
- **particularly** 副 特に, とりわけ
- **pass on** (情報などを他者に)伝える
- **pass through** 〜を経験する
- **pass ~ down** 〜を(次の世代に)伝える
- **past** 形 過去の 名 過去(の出来事)
- **path** 名 進路, 道筋
- **pattern** 名 様式, 型, 繰り返す形
- **Paul Gauguin** ポール・ゴーギャン《人名, フランスの画家。1848–1903》
- **pay** 動 〜を払う
- **Peking man** 北京原人《原始人類》
- **Pensées** 名 パンセ《著作》
- **peninsula** 名 半島
- **per** 前 〜につき, 〜ごとに
- **perhaps** 副 たぶん, ことによると
- **period** 名 期間, 時代
- **Permian Period** 二畳紀, ペルム紀
- **perspective** 名 観点
- **philosopher** 名 哲学者
- **philosophy** 名 哲学

Word List

- **phorusrhacid** 名 恐鳥類《古代生物》
- **photosynthesis** 名 光合成
- **phrase** 名 言葉, 語句
- **physical** 形 ①物理的な ②身体の, 肉体の
- **pine** 名 マツ(松)
- **pistil** 名 雌しべ
- **Pithecanthropus** 名 ピテカントロプス《原始人類》
- **place** 熟 take place 行われる, 起こる
- **plain** 名 草原
- **planetary** 形 惑星の
- **plankton** 名 プランクトン
- **plate** 名 プレート, 板状のもの
  plate tectonics プレートテクトニクス, プレート理論
- **plateau** 名 台地, 高原
- **play a part** 役目を果たす
- **player** 名 競技者, 選手
- **plenty of** たくさんの〜
- **plume** 名 煙(状の上昇[下降]流), プルーム plume tectonics プルームテクトニクス
- **plunge** 動 突っ込む
- **Pluto** 名 冥王星
- **point** 熟 up to this point これまでのところ
- **pole** 名 (南・北)極
- **pollination** 名 受粉
- **position** 名 地位, 立場
- **possess** 動 有する
- **possibility** 名 可能性
- **possible** 形 ①可能な ②ありうる, 起こりうる make it possible for 〜 to 〜が…できるようにする
- **powerful** 形 強力な, 力強い
- **Precambrian Era** 先カンブリア時代
- **precede** 動 先行する
- **predatory** 形 肉食の
- **predecessor** 名 祖先
- **prefer** 動 (〜のほうを)好む
- **prepared** 形 準備[用意]のできた
- **present** 熟 at present 今のところ, 現在は, 目下
- **preserve** 動 保持する, 守る
- **pressure** 名 圧力
- **prevent 〜 from** 〜が…できない[しない]ようにする
- **prey** 名 えじき, 食いもの 動 捕食する
- **primate** 名 霊長類
- **primitive** 形 原始の, 初期の
- **principal** 形 主な, 第一の
- **probably** 副 たぶん, あるいは
- **process** 名 ①過程, 経過 ②手順, 方法
- **progress** 名 進歩, 前進
- **property** 名 性質
- **proportion** 名 (全体に占める)割合
- **proportional** 形 比例した
- **propose** 動 提案する
- **protective** 形 保護(用)の
- **protein** 名 タンパク質
- **Proterozoic Era** 原生代
- **protozoa** 名 原生動物, 原虫
- **proud of** 《be –》〜を自慢に思う
- **prove** 動 証明する
- **provide** 動 供給する, 用意する
- **province** 名 州, 省
- **psychological** 形 精神の
- **P-T boundary** P-T境界
- **push up** 押し上げる
- **puzzle** 名 なぞ, 難問

The History of the Earth

Q
- **quake** 名 地震
- **Quaternary Period** 第四紀
- **quickly** 副 敏速に, すぐに

R
- **radiation** 名 放射能
- **radioactivity** 名 放射能[線]
- **range** 名 範囲 動 及ぶ range from ～ to ～から…に及ぶ range of ～の範囲
- **rapid** 形 急速な
- **rapidly** 副 急速に
- **rat** 名 ネズミ(鼠)
- **rate** 名 割合
- **rather** 副 むしろ, かえって rather than ～よりむしろ would rather ～する方がよい
- **ravenously** 副 貪欲に
- **ray** 名 光線, 放射線 cosmic ray 宇宙線
- **react** 動 反応する
- **reaction** 名 反応, 化学変化
- **readily** 副 すぐに
- **reality** 名 現実
- **reason** 熟 for some reason なんらかの理由で reason for ～の理由
- **reasonable** 形 筋の通った, 妥当な
- **recede** 動 ①後退する ②弱まる, 減少する
- **recent** 形 近ごろの, 近代の
- **recently** 副 近ごろ, 最近
- **record** 名 記録, 履歴
- **recover** 動 回復する
- **reduce** 動 減じる
- **reed** 名 アシ(葦)
- **reflect** 動 映る, 反映する reflect off 反射する
- **region** 名 地方, 地域
- **relationship** 名 関係
- **relative** 形 相対的な 名 同族
- **release** 動 解き放す
- **religion** 名 宗教
- **remain** 名《-s》形跡, 遺骸
- **repeat** 動 繰り返す
- **repeatedly** 副 繰り返して, たびたび
- **reproduce** 動 繁殖する
- **reproduction** 名 繁殖, 生殖
- **reptile** 名 爬虫類
- **reptilian** 形 爬虫類の
- **require** 動 必要とする, 要する
- **respiratory** 形 呼吸の
- **responsibility** 名 責任
- **rest on** ～の上に載っている
- **result** 名 結果, 成り行き 動 (結果として)起こる, 結局～になる as a result その結果(として)
- **return to** ～に戻る
- **reveal** 動 明らかにする
- **reverse** 動 逆にする, 反転する
- **revolution** 名《軸を中心にした》回転運動
- **revolve** 動《中心点の周りを》回る
- **rhythm** 名 リズム, 調子
- **rib** 名 肋骨, あばら骨
- **rigorously** 副 徹底的に
- **rise** 熟 give rise to ～を引き起こす
- **risen** 動 rise(上昇する)の過去分詞
- **RNA** 略 リボ核酸《= ribonucleic acid》
- **Rodinia** 名 ロディニア大陸《太古の大陸》
- **role** 名 役割
- **root** 名 ①根 ②《-s》先祖
- **run around** 走り回る

Word List

- **run out of** ～が不足する、～を使い果たす
- **rush** 動突進する 名殺到 **rush up to** ～に駆け上がる
- **Russia** 名ロシア《国名》

S

- **sac** 名気嚢、嚢 **air sac** 空気袋、空気嚢
- **safely** 副安全に、確実に
- **sago** 名サゴ(ヤシ) **king sago** ソテツ
- **Saturn** 名土星
- **say** 熟 **let us say** 例えば **or so it is said** そのように言われているが
- **scatter** 動ばらまく、分散する
- **sea level** 海水位
- **sea lily** ウミユリ《棘皮動物》
- **sea urchin** ウニ
- **search** 名探索、調査
- **see ～ as** ～を…と考える
- **seem** 動(～に)見える、(～のように)思われる
- **selection** 名淘汰、選抜
- **sense** 名意味
- **sentence** 名判決、宣告 **death sentence** 死刑宣告
- **separate** 動分かれる 形分かれた、別々の
- **seriously** 副深刻に、著しく
- **set loose** 放つ
- **set off** 引き起こす
- **settle** 動安定する[させる]、落ち着く **settle down** 落ち着く
- **shadow** 名影、暗がり
- **shale** 名頁岩
- **shallow** 形浅い 名《the -s》浅瀬
- **shaped like** 《be –》～のような形をしている
- **shark** 名サメ(鮫)
- **shell** 名殻、甲羅
- **shelter** 名避難所、隠れ家 **take shelter** 退避する
- **shelves** 名 shelf(棚)の複数
- **shine** 動光る、輝く
- **shore** 名岸、海岸
- **Shoshonius** 名ショショニアス《古代生物》
- **shown** 動 show(見せる)の過去分詞
- **shut** 動①閉める、閉じる ②shut の過去、過去分詞
- **Siberia** 名シベリア《地名》
- **Siberian Trap** シベリア・トラップ《洪水玄武岩の台地》
- **side** 名側、横 **either side of** ～の両側に **on either side** 両側に **side by side** 並んで
- **Silurian Period** シルル紀
- **similar** 形同じような、類似した **be similar to** ～に似ている
- **single** 形たった1つの
- **single-cell** 形単細胞の
- **sink** 動沈む、落ち込む
- **situation** 名状況、境遇
- **skull** 名頭蓋骨
- **slight** 形わずかな
- **slug** 名ナメクジ
- **snowball** 名雪玉 **Snowball Earth** 全球凍結《全表面が凍結した地球》
- **so** 熟 **and so on** ～など、その他もろもろ **or so** ～かそこらで **or so it is said** そのように言われているが **so that** ～するために、～できるように **so that** ～するために、それで、～できるように
- **society** 名社会
- **soil** 名表層土

The History of the Earth

- solar 形 太陽の solar system 太陽系
- solid 形 固体[固形]の 名 固体, 固形物
- solve 動 解く
- somehow 副 どうにかこうにか, 何とかして
- something 代 ある物, 何か have something in common 共通点がある
- sometimes 副 時々, 時には
- somewhat 副 いくらか, 多少
- somewhere 副 どこかに
- sooner or later 遅かれ早かれ
- sort out 取捨選択する
- source 名 源, 出どころ
- South America 南アメリカ, 南米
- Southeast Asia 東南アジア
- southern 形 南の
- southwest 形 南西の
- Soviet 名 旧ソヴィエト連邦, ソ連
- span 名 期間, 長さ
- specialist 名 専門家
- specialized 形 専門の, 分化した
- species 名 種, 種類
- speed 名 速力, 速度 動 急ぐ
- spiral 名 らせん
- split 動 分裂させる[する]
- sponge 名 スポンジ, 海綿
- spore 名 胞子
- spot 名 地点, 場所
- square 名 平方 1 square centimeter 1センチ平方
- stability 名 安定
- stabilize 動 安定する, 固定する
- stage 名 段階
- stamen 名 雄しべ
- standard 形 標準の

- Stanley Miller スタンリー・ミラー《人名, アメリカの化学者。1930–2007》
- start to do ~し始める
- starving 形 飢えた
- state 名 状態
- static 形 静電気の
- statistics 名 統計資料
- steadily 副 しっかりと
- steady 動 強固にする
- stem 名 茎, (木の)幹
- step forward 進み出る
- stern 形 容赦のない, 厳しい
- stir up かき混ぜる
- stone 名 石, 小石
- stop doing ~するのをやめる
- storm 名 嵐
- stove 名 こんろ, ストーブ
- strain 名 緊張, 重い負担
- stratosphere 名 成層圏
- stream 動 流れる, はためく
- strength 名 ①力, 体力 ②知力
- strengthen 動 強くする, しっかりさせる
- stretch 動 広がる 名 長さ, ひと続き
- strike 動 打ちつける, (光などが)照りつける
- striking 形 著しい, 目立つ
- string 名 一連(のもの・出来事)
- strip 動 裸にする, はぐ strip back ~をむき出しにする
- struck 動 strike (打つ)の過去, 過去分詞
- structural 形 構造(上)の
- structure 名 構造, 組織
- struggle 動 もがく, 奮闘する 名 奮闘
- Sturtian glaciation スタ―テ

Word List

ィアン氷期
- **substance** 名 物質
- **subtropical** 形 亜熱帯の
- **succeed** 動 成功する
- **success** 名 成功
- **such a** そのような
- **such as** たとえば〜、〜のような
- **such 〜 that** 非常に〜なので…
- **sudden** 形 突然の、急な
- **suffer** 動（苦痛・損害などを）受ける、こうむる
- **sufficiently** 副 十分に
- **suggest** 動 ①提唱する ②示唆する
- **sulfurous** 形 硫黄の
- **sunk** 動 sink（沈む）の過去分詞
- **supercontinent** 名 超大陸
- **super-eruption** 名 破局噴火
- **superiority** 名 優位(性)
- **supernova** 名 超新星
- **superplume** 名 スーパープルーム《マントル内の巨大な上昇流、および下降流》
- **supply** 動 供給する、補充する
- **support** 動 裏付ける
- **surely** 副 確実に
- **surface** 名 表面、水面 on the surface 外面は、表面に
- **surprising** 形 驚くべき、意外な
- **surprisingly** 副 驚いたことに
- **surround** 動 囲む、取り囲む
- **surrounding** 名《-s》周囲の状況、環境
- **survival** 名 生き残ること、生存
- **survive** 動 生き残る、存続する
- **sustain** 動 維持する、養う
- **swamp** 名 沼地、(低)湿地
- **synapsid** 単弓類、哺乳類型爬虫類
- **synthesize** 動 〜を合成する
- **system** 熟 solar system 太陽系

T

- **take** 熟 it takes 〜 to 〜の時間［労力］が必要である take a closer look より詳しく見る take a look at 〜をちょっと見る take in 取り入れる、取り込む take place 行われる、起こる take shelter 退避する
- **tantrum** 名 かんしゃく
- **tear apart** 引き裂く、分裂させる
- **technology** 名 テクノロジー、科学技術
- **tectonic plate** 構造プレート
- **tectonics** 形 構造地質学、地殻変動 plate tectonics プレートテクトニクス、プレート理論 plume tectonics プルームテクトニクス
- **teen years** 10代
- **temperature** 名 温度
- **tempestuous** 形 荒れ狂う
- **tend** 動 (〜)しがちである
- **tender** 形 優しい
- **term** 名 ①期間 ②語、用語 ③《-s》条件 come to terms with 〜と折り合いを付ける in terms of 〜を単位として、〜の観点から
- **terror bird** 恐鳥類《古代生物》
- **tested** 形 試練を経た
- **Tethys Sea** テチス海
- **th** 形 分の
- **than** 熟 more than 〜以上 rather than 〜よりむしろ than any other ほかのどの〜よりも
- **thanks to** 〜のおかげで、〜の結果
- **that** 熟 at that time その時 now that 今や〜だから、〜からには so that 〜するために、〜できるように so that 〜するために、それで、〜できるように such 〜 that 非常に〜な

111

The History of the Earth

ので…
- □ **thaw** 動 (氷・雪・霜などが) 解ける
- □ **Thecodontosaurus** 名 テコドントサウルス《恐竜》
- □ **theory** 名 理論, 学説
- □ **there** 熟 down there 下の方で[に]
- □ **therefore** 副 したがって, その結果
- □ **thick** 形 厚い, 密集した
- □ **thin** 形 薄い 動 薄くなる
- □ **think of** 〜のことを考える
- □ **this** 熟 at this time 現時点では, このとき this way このように
- □ **though** 接 〜だが, たとえ〜でも even though 〜であるけれども, 〜にもかかわらず
- □ **thousands of** 何千という
- □ **threaten** 動 脅かす, 〜の恐れがある
- □ **Thrinaxodon** 名 トリナクソドン《古代生物》
- □ **thrive** 動 繁栄する
- □ **thrown** 動 throw (投げる) の過去分詞
- □ **thunderstorm** 名 (激しい) 雷雨
- □ **Tibetan Plateau** チベット高原
- □ **time** 熟 at one time かつては at that time その時 at the time そのころ, 当時は at the time of 〜の際に at this time 現時点では, このとき for the first time 初めて in time そのうちに, やがて
- □ **tiny** 形 ちっぽけな, とても小さい
- □ **Tokyo Skytree** 東京スカイツリー《電波塔》
- □ **ton** 名 トン《重量・容積単位》
- □ **too well** 十二分に
- □ **too 〜 to** …するには〜すぎる
- □ **tool** 名 道具, 手段
- □ **torn** 動 tear (裂く) の過去分詞
- □ **tough** 形 断固たる, 乱暴な
- □ **toxic** 形 有毒な
- □ **track** 動 追跡する, たどっていく
- □ **transmit** 動 伝える, 伝わる
- □ **trap** 名 トラップ《地質構造の名称》
- □ **tremble** 動 震える 名 身震い
- □ **trial** 名 試み, 苦難
- □ **Triassic Period** 三畳紀
- □ **trick** 名 (人をだます) いたずら
- □ **trilobite** 名 三葉虫《古代生物》
- □ **truly** 副 全く, 本当に
- □ **truth** 名 事実, 真実
- □ **tsunami** 名 津波
- □ **turn** 熟 as it turned out 後でわかったことだが turn into 〜に変わる turn out (結局〜に) なる turn the clock back 時計を巻き戻す turn to 〜に変わる turn white 白くなる
- □ **turtle** 名 ウミガメ (海亀)
- □ **typhoon** 名 台風
- □ **Tyrannosaurus** 名 ティラノサウルス《恐竜》

U

- □ **ultraviolet** 形 紫外線の
- □ **unbelievably** 副 信じられないほど
- □ **unbroken** 形 (記録などが) 破られていない
- □ **uncertain** 形 不確かな
- □ **uncertainty** 名 不確かさ, 不確定要素
- □ **unclear** 形 はっきりしない
- □ **undergo** 動 経験する, 被る
- □ **underground** 形 地下の [にある] 名 地下
- □ **underwent** 動 undergo (経験する) の過去
- □ **unit** 名 構成単位

Word List

- **universal** 形 宇宙の
- **universe** 名《the - /the U-》宇宙, 全世界
- **unknown** 形 未知の, 解明されていない
- **unprecedented** 形 空前の, 未曾有の
- **unrest** 名 不安, 動揺
- **up to** ~まで, ~に至るまで
- **up to this point** これまでのところ
- **upon** 前 ①《場所・接触》~(の上)に ②~に関して, ~について
- **upper** 形 上の, 上位の
- **Uranus** 名 天王星
- **urchin** 名 ハリネズミ sea urchin ウニ
- **use** 熟 make use of ~を利用する, ~を生かす used to ①以前は~だった ②《be/get -》~に慣れる

V

- **validate** 動 正当と認める
- **vapor** 名 蒸気, 気体
- **vaporize** 動 蒸発する
- **variety** 名 種類, 型
- **various** 形 変化に富んだ, さまざまの
- **vast** 形 広大な, 巨大な
- **vegetation** 名 植物
- **vent** 名 穴 volcanic vent 火道《マグマの通り道》
- **Venus** 名 金星
- **vertebra** 名 脊椎骨, 背骨
- **vertebrae** 名 vertebra (脊椎骨)の複数
- **vertebrate** 名 脊椎動物
- **violent** 形 激しい, 強烈な
- **volcanic** 形 ①火山の ②強烈な
- volcanic vent 火道《マグマの通り道》
- **volcano** 名 火山, 噴火口
- **volt** 名 ボルト《電圧単位》
- **Vredefort Dome** フレデフォート・ドーム《隕石衝突跡》
- **vulnerable** 形 被害に遭いやすい, 脆弱な

W

- **Wales** 名 ウェールズ《英国南西部の地方》
- **wander** 動 歩き回る
- **warming** 名 温暖化, 温度上昇
- **wave** 名 波
- **wavelength** 名 波長
- **way** 熟 by the way ところで, ついでに make one's way 進む, 行く on the way 途中で this way このように way of life 暮らし方 way to ~する方法
- **weaken** 動 弱くなる, 弱める
- **weapon** 名 武器, 兵器
- **weigh** 動 重さが~ある
- **weight** 名 重さ
- **well** 熟 as well as ~と同様に do well 栄える too well 十二分に
- **whale** 名 クジラ (鯨)
- **whatever** 代 どんなこと[もの]が~とも
- **whenever** 接 ~するたびに
- **whether** 接 ~かどうか, ~であろうとなかろうと
- **white** 熟 turn white 白くなる
- **whole** 名《the -》全体, 全部 as a whole 全体として
- **whom** 代《関係代名詞》~するところの人
- **wide** 形 幅広い, 広範囲の

The History of the Earth

- **widely** 副 広範囲にわたって
- **wing** 名 翼, 羽
- **wipe** 動 ぬぐう, ふきとる **wipe off** 拭い去る **wipe out** 一掃する, 全滅させる
- **wisdom** 名 知恵
- **within** 前 ～の中［内］に, ～の内部に
- **wolf** 名 オオカミ（狼）
- **word** 熟 **in other words** すなわち, 言い換えれば
- **worry about** ～のことを心配する
- **worsen** 動 悪化する［させる］
- **worst** 形 《the –》最も悪い, いちばんひどい **worst of all** 一番困るのは, 最悪なことに
- **worth** 形 ～に価する
- **would rather** ～する方がよい

X, Y

- **X-ray** 名 《しばしば -s》X線
- **year** 熟 **for years** 何年も **teen years** 10代
- **Yellow River** 黄河
- **yet** 熟 **not yet** まだ～してない
- **Yucatán Peninsula** ユカタン半島
- **Yunnan** 雲南《地名》

114

English Conversational Ability Test
国際英語会話能力検定

● E-CATとは…
英語が話せるようになるためのテストです。インターネットベースで、30分であなたの発話力をチェックします。

www.ecatexam.com

● iTEP®とは…
世界各国の企業、政府機関、アメリカの大学300校以上が、英語能力判定テストとして採用。オンラインによる90分のテストで文法、リーディング、リスニング、ライティング、スピーキングの5技能をスコア化。iTEP®は、留学、就職、海外赴任などに必要な、世界に通用する英語力を総合的に評価する画期的なテストです。

www.itepexamjapan.com

ラダーシリーズ
The History of the Earth 地球の歴史

2018年7月8日　第1刷発行

著　者　西海コエン

発行者　浦　晋亮

発行所　IBCパブリッシング株式会社
　　　　〒162-0804 東京都新宿区中里町29番3号
　　　　菱秀神楽坂ビル9F
　　　　Tel. 03-3513-4511　Fax. 03-3513-4512
　　　　www.ibcpub.co.jp

© Coen Nishiumi 2018
© IBC Publishing, Inc. 2018

印刷　中央精版印刷株式会社
装丁　伊藤 理恵　　カバー写真　Triff / Shutterstock.com
組版データ　Sabon Roman + Source Sans Pro Bold

落丁本・乱丁本は、小社宛にお送りください。送料小社負担にてお取り替えいたします。本書の無断複写(コピー)は著作権法上での例外を除き禁じられています。

Printed in Japan
ISBN978-4-7946-0547-4